Unbroken

Journey through love and loss

Esther N. Wafula

Dedication

To my beloved children: Ethan, Elsa, Hadasha, and my precious heavenly angel Elna. My entire existence has revolved around you. You have shown me what true strength and resilience mean.

Acknowledgment

I want to thank my heavenly grandparents and my dear parents. Thank you for giving me an indomitable spirit and longevity genes. Dad, you believed in the power of transformation and honesty. Mama, I have yet to meet a soul as gentle yet resilient as yours.

To all my siblings, thank you for being my best friends. You have always had my back.

To my children, thank you for your endless love and kisses. My motherhood is a rainbow, full of vibrant colors and sparkle.

To my one and only, thank you for choosing me as your sole and exclusive priority.

To my publishing team, I greatly appreciate the effort put into transforming my thoughts into a book. The process was undoubtedly challenging, as I experienced firsthand. The continuous stream of phone calls, suggestions, and guidance throughout this journey has been invaluable.

Above all, I want to thank my God. You have bestowed upon me life and strength. I am still amazed by all the miracles that have unfolded in my life. There are no limits to what can be achieved in your name.

About the Author

Esther, a veterinary medicine graduate from the University of Nairobi and the University of Utrecht, was raised in rural Africa before moving to Middlesex, New Jersey. Despite encountering obstacles such as cancer, depression, amnesia, and losing her corporate job, she persisted and now works full-time in corporate America. She is also an emerging real estate investor and a proud mother of four, although she recently suffered the heartbreaking loss of her teenage daughter. She finds solace in her passions, exploring new destinations and enjoying diverse cuisines. Esther's memoir serves as a beacon of hope, reminding us that even in adversity, the human spirit can triumph.

Contents

Chapter 1: The Beginning

EVERY STORY BEGINS SOMEWHERE, and while I may not have the ending figured out yet, I know exactly where my journey began. I knew where I came from and what country I was born in, but I never knew how big I could get.

My story began with my birth and birthplace. I was born in Eastern Africa, in the heart of a quaint tiny village nestled in the heart of Western Kenya, in the late 1970s. Far from the hustle and bustle of modern living, life in the village was unlike anything else. Yet, it offered me a chance to understand the world around me, the struggles of my people, and the determination to carve out a better future.

Back then, our village was a humble place, laden with dirt roads and no modern conveniences or amenities like electricity or paved streets. We did not have running water or indoor toilets. Ours was a simple life, with toilets or out-backs situated away from the main houses, accessible only by dirt paths. Despite this lack of facilities, life in our underdeveloped village had its charm.

Our days were filled with twelve hours of work, followed by twelve hours of relaxation under the starry night sky. Each day would begin with the rising sun casting a golden glow upon the thatched roofs of our cottages. Like most families, we would set out to tend to our fields and livestock, working diligently for twelve hours under the warm embrace of the sun. As the evening descended, signaling the end of another day's toil, a sense of tranquility would descend upon the Village. The evenings were enchanting. Without any interference from artificial lights or pollution to obscure the splendor of the stars overhead, the night sky sparkled. We would come together as kids, admiring the patterns of the constellations and sharing our hopes with each passing shooting star, as we made our wishes.

Time was measured not by the ticking of clocks but by the sun's journey across the sky from dawn to dusk. As villagers, we lived in perfect harmony with nature, following the rhythms of the earth and sky.

As a young girl in Africa during that era, I faced challenges, but I found a deep reservoir of strength inside me that could not be extinguished. Poverty was a constant presence, casting a shadow over every aspect of life. Access to medical care was a distant hope for most, beyond their financial reach. Navigating a society steeped in patriarchal customs and polygamous traditions was a daunting task for a girl like me. Women carried the weight of these societal expectations, often pushed to the sidelines and silenced.

Despite the challenges, I found happiness and cherished every moment, thriving on the simple joys of life - the warmth of my family, the wonders of nature, and the shared moments under the celestial canopy.

I came into existence on a cold evening during the late 1970s. Back then, there were no luxurious maternity hospitals or advanced facilities for women during childbirth. Expectant mothers depended on themselves and the women in their community for assistance. They either gave birth on their own or with the help of any willing helpers or doulas. As the mother cried out in pain, the supportive women sang ancient melodies to alleviate her suffering, serving as her form of anesthesia.

The arrival of my birth brought immense joy and celebration to my entire family. Having previously endured the devastating loss of two children to infant mortality, my parents and the rest of the family were overwhelmed with happiness to finally welcome a healthy baby into their lives. My birth brought a profound sense of relief, especially considering the lack of advanced maternity hospitals or modern facilities available during that time. The wave of relief and happiness that swept over everyone was indescribable. In keeping with our family's tradition, I was given the name of my paternal grandmother, honoring her legacy and connecting me to my roots.

From my earliest memories, I witnessed the heartbreaking reality of infant deaths in my village. It was a solemn truth that we became familiar with at a young age, knowing all too well the constant battle to keep the babies alive amidst what we called the "infant curse." However, I take comfort in the knowledge that, in recent times, there has been a significant decrease in the rates of infant mortality throughout the African continent.

The improvement in the situation can be attributed to various factors, such as economic development, increased access to nutritious food, enhanced knowledge about newborn care, higher hygiene standards, and, most significantly, advancements in healthcare practices. In the past, diseases like malaria and poor sanitation contributed to alarming rates of infant mortality. The absence of proper maternity services added to the risks faced by mothers and their babies. Often, women had to manage childbirth alone, resorting to using unsterilized tools like rusty knives or razor blades to cut the umbilical cord.

In our own home, I experienced firsthand the challenges of childbirth when my mother gave birth to my younger brother all by herself. I was just five years old at the time, and it all happened so quickly. My mother ventured out into the bushes behind our house, armed with nothing but a piece of cloth and a sharp razor.

With the cloth, she carefully wrapped the newborn, and with the razor, she skillfully cut the umbilical cord and safely delivered the baby into her arms. We anxiously waited, and soon enough, we heard the cry of the newborn. In the blink of an eye, my younger brother came into the world under the humblest circumstances. It was a stark reminder of the realities of life in rural Kenya, where access to medical care and assistance during childbirth was scarce.

I remember many unsafe and unhygienic practices passed off as medical interventions in those early days. Plagued by the constant threat of malaria, ignorance led to some dangerous practices parading as medical solutions. A group of individuals claimed to be experts in malaria prevention, offering their services without any legitimate credentials.

These self-proclaimed healers would move from door to door, armed with mysterious potions and remedies they guaranteed would ward off the deadly disease. The villagers, desperate for protection, welcomed these interventions without question. The adults allowed these groups to use the same needles to administer the supposed prophylaxis after boiling some water. This blind trust might have resulted from a lack of education, making it simpler for people to believe in the effectiveness of the supposed malaria treatment.

Unexpected consequences resulted from these unsanitary practices. Following the treatment, we experienced discomfort and were unable to sit comfortably for a week due to nursing abscesses.

From my earliest memories, the echoes of polygamy and patriarchal structures reverberated through the community, shaping lives and destinies, and they continue to persist to this day. Under patriarchal rule, a man, as the head of the family, held all the authority. Presiding over households with firm hands and even firmer beliefs. The more wives a man possessed, the greater his status in the eyes of his peers. In this world, tradition held sway over modernity, and polygamy found fertile ground to flourish.

Polygamy was originally intended to offer extra assistance to the primary wife by marrying additional wives, whether it be a second, third, fourth, or even fifth wife, especially for affluent men with means. These subsequent unions were less about enjoyment and more about ensuring the welfare of numerous women and their families. The wives would divide household tasks and duties amongst themselves while their husbands ensured their livelihood.

I grew up in a similar polygamous family, where my siblings and I were the youngest members of the household. Living in a polygamous family had its fair share of challenges. While others in similar circumstances clung tightly to traditional beliefs, my father broke free from these constraints and embraced the power of education to shape our destinies. Unlike many others, he wholeheartedly believed in the power of education. He tirelessly emphasized the importance of learning, encouraging us to immerse ourselves in books and seek knowledge beyond the boundaries of our homes. Despite the murmurs of dissent from extended family members who believed in upholding age-old customs of not educating girls, my father remained resolute.

As I reflect on my upbringing, I am reminded of the profound influence my father had on me. His guidance not only molded me into the person I am today, but also steered me towards my career path. With a strong foundation built on vision and unwavering commitment, he dedicated himself tirelessly to his work as an animal health technician.

I have such great memories of going with him as he made his rounds on different animal farms in our village. Watching him identify illnesses and care for the animals really stuck with me. It was during these moments that I found my true calling. My father's down-to-earth attitude and modesty shone through in how he approached his work and everyday life. He had this amazing ability to connect with both animals and humans, showing care and respect for each. His innovative problem-solving skills on the farms, despite having limited equipment and medical supplies, motivated me to be creative in my own pursuits.

As I grew up, my father was dubbed "the Bismarck of Germany" by the villagers - a title that echoed both his intellect and shrewd business acumen. His quiet demeanor belied his sharp mind, and every decision he made was like a meticulously planned play on a chessboard, earning him consistent success.

Also, he was someone everyone in the village looked up to for advice, knowing that his guidance was always practical and effective. The villagers admired him not only for his success but for his unwavering integrity. When faced with dilemmas, my father would retreat into thoughtful silence, emerging with solutions that always carried the day.

Despite his reserved nature, my father treasured the friendships he cultivated. His inner circle knew him as a man of few words but endless wisdom. He was that pillar that the people trusted and leaned on in times of uncertainty for advice and guidance. I often marveled at the way he navigated through life like a master strategist playing a grand game. His legacy was not just in the wealth he amassed but in the lives he touched, and the hearts he inspired. It is hardly surprising that many individuals back then, and in future generations, desired to relate to his name.

As a child, I was fortunate to enjoy good health, aside from the occasional bouts of malaria or fever. Our village was a haven where children could roam freely without fear. We attended school together, played in the fields, and helped tend to the family farms. Our community was a tight-knit one, where everyone knew each other and looked out for one another. There was a keen sense of unity and mutual respect among the villagers. In contrast to the present world, where dangers seem to be lurking around every corner, our village provided us with a comforting shield of protection. Safety was a given, and the idea of kidnappings or predators preying on children was unheard of in those days. We wandered without worry, going about our daily tasks and enjoying our playtime without a care in the world.

Growing up in a rather privileged environment, I couldn't help but feel grateful for the abundance of blessings in my life. Yet, I couldn't ignore the stark differences that existed among my peers, particularly when it came to something as fundamental as footwear. While I had the luxury of having shoes for school, it saddened me to see many of my classmates unable to afford them. In order to avoid drawing attention to myself, I got into the habit of taking off my shoes before stepping into school. Going barefoot was my way of fitting in with everyone else. It wasn't until I left school that I would slyly put my boots back on. This simple act was my way of steering clear of any possible bullying, teasing, or feeling left out.

In my early years, there was a teacher who played a significant role in shaping my life. She recognized my immense potential and went above and beyond to motivate and back me up. Not only did she have conversations with my father about my abilities, but she also convinced him to make a valuable investment in my education. As a result, when I reached fourth grade, I had the privilege of attending a prestigious girls' boarding school.

Stepping into this unfamiliar school brought a mix of excitement and nervousness. The thought of donning the fresh uniforms and shoes filled me with joy, knowing that I didn't have to conform by taking them off. My trusty metal case became my faithful companion, safeguarding all my treasured possessions.

The initial thrill waned as a wave of homesickness washed over me. I longed for my parents and siblings with an ache that seemed unbearable, and the school's meager food portions left me in a constant state of hunger. Each month's end brought a surge of anticipation as I eagerly awaited my parents' arrival, treasuring every precious moment spent together. These visits were a balm for both my family and me, offering a welcome escape from the hardships of being far from home. And to my delight, they often brought along homemade dishes for us to relish.

At my brand-new boarding school, it was customary for the older students to take on the responsibility of introducing the newcomers and assisting them in getting accustomed to the environment. Fortunately, I had the advantage of having my stepsister already studying there, which meant I didn't require anyone else's guidance. Nevertheless, our relationship was not the best, and I ended up doing her chores without much appreciation in return.

As the older students took charge of showing the newcomers around the school, I found myself in a unique predicament. Instead of receiving a warm welcome or a tour guide, I became an unwilling participant in her school tasks. I found myself at her beck and call, fetching items, doing her laundry, and being met with scorn in return. The initial excitement of a new school quickly faded into resentment. I questioned my decision to enroll at this particular institution as I drowned in my stepsister's demands.

In spite of the challenges and the burdens placed upon me, I began to find my place within the school community. By the time I reached sixth grade, I had made genuine friendships and excelled in my academics. The boarding school that once seemed like a burden had become a place of growth and opportunity.

Transitioning to high school at the age of twelve was both nerve-wracking and exciting. The journey from my village to the school felt like it took forever, with multiple bus connections along the dusty roads. Enrolling in an all-girls high school was not much different from my previous experience, but it still felt like a significant milestone.

My dad being there with me on the first day of school, paying my tuition meant the world to me. His support and encouragement really boosted my confidence to tackle whatever high school threw my way.

My high school experience was unforgettable, brimming with fresh challenges and chances for personal development. It was in those years that I started to grasp the importance of addressing gender-related issues concerning women, all thanks to our encouraging yet strict teachers. The knowledge I gained in high school proved to be essential as I ventured into college and the future.

From the very beginning, joining both the hockey team and the drama club during my high school journey was an absolute thrill. It had been a long-standing desire of mine, and finally being able to immerse myself in activities that truly ignited my passion brought me an overwhelming sense of happiness. Looking forward to school days became a breeze knowing that I would have the opportunity to actively participate in these incredible endeavors. I was also a part of the music club. Performing in concerts and competitions allowed me to express myself musically while bonding with friends. These extracurricular activities added a whole new dimension to my high school experience, making each day more exciting and fulfilling.

High school is more than just hitting the books; it's a transformative period where students shape their outlooks and experience substantial personal growth. For numerous students, high school acts as a springboard for profound development that influences their future years. It serves as a central platform for contemplating career paths, whether one aspires to attend college, enter the workforce, or embark on the journey of marriage.

Personally, I discovered that navigating through high school can be quite demanding due to its short academic periods. With only three months of school followed by a month-long break for holidays, mastering the art of time management became crucial in preparing for what lay ahead.

During holidays, I pitched in with household chores, helped out on the family farm, and looked after my younger siblings. Though challenging, these experiences taught me valuable skills like problem-solving, teamwork, and resilience.

As a young girl in a countryside village, my journey through adolescence was filled with unique obstacles due to attending an all-girls school. From navigating the complexities of relationships with boys to grasping the intricacies of menstrual cycles amidst societal pressures, every day presented fresh challenges that I had to conquer. Despite that, my home was filled with teenagers my age who often acted as a sounding board for me. Our doors were always open to strangers and individuals seeking assistance, whether it be a warm meal, a place to sleep, or support for their children's education.

Thanks to my family's financial resources, we were able to give back to those in need. My father, a strong advocate for equal educational opportunities, made sure that children from underprivileged backgrounds had a safe place to stay and access to basic schooling.

While most fathers in our village believed that a girl's place was in the kitchen, my father believed in the power of education. Many fathers did not value girls' education, they believed that women were born to be homemakers. According to them, girls were raised to look after their homes, husbands, and families, and that did not require an education.

As much as education was considered unnecessary for girls, it was believed that educated girls would struggle to find suitable matches. The elders preached that no man desired an opinionated wife whose thoughts had been tainted by the influence of the White man's education.

The situation was worsened by the fact that the few educated women who could have served as role models were either divorced or had suffered some form of domestic violence, facing severe criticism from society. Occasionally, their battered faces and torn spirits would make headlines in the local newspapers. Any woman who dared to defy societal norms and pursue education would be met with disapproval and whispers of condemnation at every turn. The elders would shake their heads in disappointment, cautioning that educated women were destined for a life of solitude and hardship, pointing to the silent heroines who had endured abuse in silence.

Also, there was this prevailing notion that educating girls was a fruitless endeavor. Families hesitated to invest in their daughters' education, fearing that the girls would grow too independent and not heed their future husbands if they were lucky to find a match. It was widely believed that any educational benefits would be reaped solely by the husbands, rendering girls' education a poor investment.

However, in this village lived a man unlike the others. He was a strong advocate for girl-child education and firmly believed in the power of knowledge for all. That man was my father. Despite facing criticism and skepticism, he stood unwavering in his support for educating girls.

In addition to his passion for education, he showed a strong commitment to our academic success. Each year, at the beginning and end of the school year, my dad would gather us kids to discuss our progress, challenges, areas needing improvement, and strategies for doing better in the upcoming year. He was even willing to invest in private tutors if needed.

As I sit here, reminiscing while I pen down this memoir, I am instantly transported back to the tranquil setting of my father's study. The gentle radiance emanating from an age-old oil lamp envelops the room, casting a comforting glow on the walls, setting the stage for my father to impart his wisdom to me and my siblings. As we listened intently, his voice flowed like a steady river, leading us with an abundance of wisdom and knowledge while sprinkling captivating anecdotes along the way. Each word he uttered resonated deeply, revealing a man who had graduated from the school of life lessons; he truly understood the significance of life, friendship, investing, education, and self-reliance.

He consistently stressed the significance of education, striving to be better and aiming for the stars no matter how distant they seemed. But it was not just about academic success; it was about being self-sufficient, about standing on your own two feet and facing the challenges of the world head-on.

This is something I have carried with me, and I use the same technique with my kids to discuss their academics and life challenges.

My mother was a resolute teacher and specialized in teaching young students in elementary and middle school. In those days, they were known as P1 teachers, although I'm uncertain if the same term is used here in the USA. She dedicated her skills to our primary section, where she taught students from grades one to eight. After two years of professional teaching, she made the choice to prioritize raising our family on a full-time basis.

My mother possessed a heart of gold that extended far beyond her role as a teacher. She consistently displayed her generosity by lending a helping hand to those in need and offering support to the less fortunate in our community. Among her many passions, she found great fulfillment in providing shelter and nourishment to those who required assistance.

Moreover, my mother spearheaded a grassroots campaign within our neighborhood. She diligently put together compact packages and baskets filled with essential items for expectant mothers or new moms who were facing financial hardships. Personally, delivering these thoughtful care packages to these families was her heartfelt way of extending a helping hand and spreading compassion to those who needed it the most. This selfless act of kindness truly made a lasting impression on the women in our community.

Growing up in a family of seven, my parents always made sure we had more than enough resources to thrive. We had our own cattle, which provided us with fresh milk that not only nourished our family but also enabled us to lend a helping hand to those in need by sharing and selling it. The best part is, we never had to fret about allergies or illnesses that often come with store-bought milk. Even now, the delightful taste of fresh milk brings back cherished memories from my childhood.

My family was fortunate to have a vast expanse of fertile land spanning twenty-seven acres, nestled alongside a creek that locals affectionately called a river. Those were the days when my siblings and I would gleefully splash around in the water, catching fish and creating cherished memories. Our land was not only a source of joy but also a means of sustenance, as we diligently cultivated grains, beans, and vegetables that provided the essential staples for our household. We took pride in consuming the fruits of our labor and even sold the surplus to generate extra income.

Moreover, my parents owned a fleet of mini-buses and minivans, which they skillfully operated to transport passengers throughout our village. As the sun set, I would observe my mother diligently overseeing the financial affairs of our transportation business. She would handle cash, distribute wages to the drivers and assistants, and meticulously maintain records. It was interesting to note that during those times, people had a peculiar habit of keeping their money at home instead of depositing it in the nearby Barclays Bank. This tradition had been passed down through generations, as they believed their money was safer behind their own walls. Despite the grandeur of the bank, the people valued the secrecy and security provided by their own homes.

My family not only engaged in agricultural and transportation activities, but we also ran a milling business. This business involved processing corn into flour and other delicious maize-based food products that people could enjoy.

I have a clear memory of observing customers as they brought in their maize to be milled. Every customer's maize was carefully weighed, and payment was collected upfront before the milling process commenced. The collected money was then recorded and utilized to efficiently compensate the shop's employees and ensure smooth business operations. Being immersed in such entrepreneurial activities during my upbringing greatly shaped my perspective on entrepreneurship.

Growing up in a family where resourcefulness was key, being the oldest child meant taking on a leadership role early on. Even now, that "oldest child syndrome" is a part of who I am. I had to ensure everyone completed their chores and that my younger siblings were well taken care of - bathed, cleaned, and dressed in clean clothes.

We were also required to sweep the house so our parents would return home to a tidy house and prepare the vegetables for dinner. Cornmeal was a staple food in our household, so we would always add some vegetables or meat to switch up the flavors every night.

As a young girl, I took on these responsibilities without any trouble, but I had bigger plans for myself than just tending to my siblings and maintaining the house. I was curious about the world and what lay outside the physical boundaries of my village.

Every time an airplane flew over our house, I would go to my dad and ask him questions about it. He never missed a beat and would always answer any question that I had. When I was young, he shared his knowledge of the world with me, which opened up the biosphere for me and instilled an even greater curiosity in me to experience all of it for myself.

Growing up, my parents had a unique parenting style - they were both open and supportive yet had their fair share of restrictions. Visiting our extended family was one aspect where they were particularly stringent. I couldn't quite understand their reasons for being so protective, but it only made me more curious about the mysterious world that lay beyond our usual boundaries.

Each time we had the chance to visit our relatives, they would graciously spread-out rugs and mats on the floor, offering us a place to rest as their homes lacked proper sleeping arrangements. With no blankets or covers to shield us from the biting cold, we had to rely solely on the warmth of our own garments. This eye-opening encounter humbled me, revealing the diverse levels of poverty and scarcity that existed within Africa, truths that had been shielded from my awareness until that moment. Despite the restrictions, I learned to appreciate the occasional family gatherings even more. Out of all those cherished experiences, my fondest memory was the time we paid a visit to my maternal grandmother.

Christmas has always been the highlight of my childhood, and to this day, it remains my absolute favorite time of the year. It was such a magical occasion where we would all dress up in brand-new clothes and shoes, looking our very best before heading to church for the festivities. I can still vividly recall the excitement of writing poems to recite during the Christmas service, adding to the already joyous atmosphere.

During the festive Christmas season, our community had a special gentleman who played a crucial part in immortalizing our cherished moments. He skillfully captured our family gatherings through his photography, offering his services for a fee. Despite the wait for the Polaroid printouts, the excitement of seeing the final results was always worth it. These photographs truly captured the essence of our happiest times together, becoming precious keepsakes that we still treasure dearly.

It was a beloved tradition within our family, filling our hearts with happiness and warmth each and every year. Every family member would make the journey back home for this special occasion, and it consistently spanned an entire week of pure jubilation. There was always cooking, baking, singing Christmas carols, and the younger ones would proudly showcase their new outfits and shoes.

In Africa, our large family still comes together at our parents' house every Christmas, keeping alive the beloved customs we've treasured for generations. It's amazing to see how my brothers have passed on these traditions to their own families, making our celebrations even more special. With the help of technology, we can now video call and spread the holiday cheer.

It is important to highlight the significance of my grandparents, especially my paternal grandparents, whom I never had the opportunity to meet as they had already departed from this world. I discovered that my grandfather used to toil as a general laborer for the colonial masters, even working in their kitchen. During those times, being employed by the white man was considered a privilege. This occupation paved the way for my father and his siblings to attain an education and acquire valuable skills of reading and writing.

My dad chose to become an animal health technician and trained under a skilled white veterinary doctor. Even when he returned back to England, he kept in touch with his mentee. Interestingly, I received a copy of my father's farewell letter from the 1960s through Jack Hammonds, my dad's previous boss. Although we never had the chance to meet in person, we exchanged letters. I was amazed by the flawless English in my dad's letter - it was truly amazing.

I comprehend that my paternal grandmother engaged in trading. She cultivated crops and was involved in sales. She held the position of the sole wife in the family, through all the years. My grandfather never took on another wife, he stayed loyal to her. They were blessed with seven children, one of whom is my father. While I may not have all the details, I do know that one of my uncles valiantly served in the great World War II. It is truly remarkable that every member of my dad's family was fortunate enough to inherit favorable genes, allowing them to relish a long and fulfilling life.

In contrast, my mother originated from a complex polygamous household. They were so impoverished and relied on the land for sustenance. Eventually, my mother found herself residing with a prosperous uncle, which granted her the opportunity to receive an education. On the other hand, my maternal grandmother faced difficulties in making ends meet, yet she compensated for the lack of material possessions with her spirituality. She devoutly recited the rosary throughout the day and night.

Additionally, she engaged in the production of corn liquor for commercial purposes. Unfortunately, they encountered legal troubles and were often apprehended for their involvement in the production of corn liquor, resulting in substantial monetary penalties. Despite these challenges, both my grandmother and grandfather possessed a profound love for their grandchildren.

While penning this memoir, I would frequently find myself reaching for the weathered photographs of my parents. They have both departed from this world, with my father living a long life until the age of ninety-one. I am filled with gratitude and empowerment.

I am aware that I can document and narrate my tale, one that exemplifies grit, perseverance, and liberation.

Looking back now, I realize that my father may have seen something the rest of us had not. He may have sensed the shifting tides of the world, the subtle changes that were beginning to take root. Perhaps he knew that a new era was dawning, where women would no longer be confined to the roles society had assigned them.

As I pondered his words, I could not help but wonder if my father had foreseen a world where women would have the power to shape their destinies to break free from the chains of tradition and expectation. A world where they could step into the light, strong and independent, ready to conquer whatever lay ahead. A world where they could stand tall, feed themselves and their families, and make their mark.

And so, armed with the lessons my father had taught me, I ventured forth into this brave new world. It would be a world where women could stand tall, provide for themselves and their families, and leave behind anything that held them back. Because of him, I was ready to embrace the future, carve out my path, and make my mark on the world in a way that would have made him proud.

As I reminisce about my mother, I am reminded of her constant smile and the immense love and wisdom she showered upon me. Her selflessness knew no bounds, as she would have willingly sacrificed her own life for any of her children. Even on her deathbed, amidst the preparations for a kidney transplant in a distant land, she remained steadfast in imparting her knowledge without a hint of complaint. When the social worker mentioned that her time was limited, a part of me refused to believe it. I silently thought to myself, "they simply don't understand the strength of my mother." She was a force to be reckoned with yet possessed a gentle and compassionate soul. Sadly, she passed away, leaving an immense void in my heart.

People often say that time heals, but in that moment of loss, those words felt hollow and empty.

I am who I am today, and I could not be more thrilled about my identity. The values of kindness, honesty, and hard work were instilled in me by my parents, who always emphasized the importance of extending a helping hand to others. Their guidance and teachings have played a significant role in shaping me into the woman I am today, and for that, I am truly grateful for my upbringing.

Chapter 2: The Later Years

LIFE IS UNPREDICTABLE, and you never know who you will meet and how they'll impact your journey. Sometimes, we meet people who come into our lives and change them forever. Sometimes, the change is for the better, but sometimes it is the opposite. Each encounter teaches us something valuable, leaving a lasting memory etched in our hearts.

Writing about my life has always been a challenge. I may never be able to put into words the emotions, experiences, and lessons that I have gone through. When it comes to my husband, it feels like I could write a whole book just about him because he's been such a significant part of my story. Nevertheless, here I am, attempting to capture his essence in just a few words, hoping to convey the depth of our experience together as best as I can.

Life has a funny way of unfolding, doesn't it?? Fate has a way of surprising us when we least expect it. Meeting my husband was like something out of a dream. It was love at first sight, but reality soon set in, and I realized what I had gotten myself into.

It was during my college days when our paths crossed, all thanks to a mutual friend. The memory is still vivid in my mind like it happened just yesterday. It was a regular day, walking towards a nearby shopping center from my hostel. When I saw my friend, her nervousness was palpable. Intrigued, I went up to her, only to find out she was about to meet someone who had caught her interest. Without a second thought, I gave her a reassuring smile and said, "Don't worry, I've got your back.".

With my unwavering support, I was able to instantly ease her worries. The look of relief that swept across her face was truly invaluable, as she realized she wouldn't have to confront the situation all by herself.

The moment the man arrived, I couldn't help but feel taken aback by his presence. He was a tall and shy guy who checked off all the right boxes. There was a certain allure about him that captivated my attention. However, despite my initial attraction, I knew I had to restrain myself due to his interest in my friend. Yet, as they conversed, my friend disclosed that she had moved on from him since their last encounter and was now expecting a child with someone else.

He was completely unaware of what was to come, his expression shifting to one of disappointment as he noticed my friend's growing baby bump. This unexpected meeting turned out to be the start of my adventure with the man who would soon become my husband.! Although there was an undeniable chemistry that simmered between us, he didn't confess his feelings until later on. I kept my composure, telling myself that he was simply a friend of a friend. That evening, we swapped numbers, and from then on, our chats evolved and flourished into a series of delightful, casual dates.

When we crossed paths, he had a decade of life experience on me, while I was merely a twenty-year-old. It was during a phase in my life when I realized that I desired a companion who possessed wisdom and stability, someone who could make wise choices and had a clear direction for their future. Discovering him felt like stumbling upon the ideal match I had been yearning for.

Naturally, I could not wait to embark on this journey and see where our relationship would lead us.

As our bond strengthened, he introduced me to his twins, a boy and a girl. He was single-handedly raising them with the assistance of a live-in nanny. Witnessing their joy in having a maternal figure in their lives made me understand the profoundness of our relationship. This realization was a factor in my choice to fully invest in the relationship, although I recognized the importance of discussing it with my parents before moving forward.

Bringing up the twins at first presented a significant challenge. Despite my youth, I found myself abruptly faced with the duties of motherhood and had to figure out how to divide my time and attention between the two. I recalled the skills I had acquired from looking after my younger siblings, which proved to be quite useful. My mother was always just a phone call away, ready to offer guidance whenever I struggled with this new responsibility. Despite the obstacles, I took comfort in the fact that they were lovely children who exhibited exceptional discipline and affection, underscoring their need for a mother's love and care.

Growing up, I always told my parents they would be the first to know if I found the guy of my dreams. Little did I know that it would happen one day. So, when I finally found him, we decided to travel to my parents' house in the village and introduce him to them. We were both nervous about how they would respond, but we knew it was important for them to meet him.

The look of astonishment on his face was undeniable as he witnessed me being unabashedly candid with my father. In a society deeply rooted in tradition and patriarchal norms, it was uncommon for girls to display such freedom of expression, especially with their fathers. Growing up, women were expected to be seen and not heard, to conform to societal expectations of docility and compliance.

However, my relationship with my father was different. We shared a bond that transcended conventional roles; we were more like friends than father and daughter. Our connection was built on mutual respect, trust, and open communication. I felt comfortable sharing my thoughts and opinions with him, knowing that he would listen without judgment and respond with understanding.

Despite that, the introduction was a success. My husband, who is warm and friendly, effortlessly charmed my parents. They embraced him warmly, and we had a delightful evening together. My mother, true to form, was gracious and accepting towards him, putting my mind at ease. Meanwhile, my father reminded me that I needed to finish college before tying the knot in a traditional white wedding. That was the promise I gave my father at that time, but as life is unpredictable, you never know what will throw your way, so always be prepared for anything.

On our way back from the village, we faced a twelve-hour journey to return to the city where my college was located. Since it was a long trip, we decided to rest overnight and continue our journey in the morning.

I recall telling my husband, "Make sure we're back by eight o'clock. I can't afford to miss my exam tomorrow."

He assured me, "Don't worry, I'm going to do that," and he continued driving.

The next morning, as we resumed our journey, everything seemed to be going smoothly until suddenly, we swerved off the road and collided with something. There was a loud crash, and our car began rolling over and over. In the chaos of the moment, I realized my husband was no longer in control, and it dawned on me that this might be our last moment together. The confusion of the situation made it hard to remember exactly what happened next.

The car abruptly halted, and then an eerie silence enveloped everything. When I woke up, it seemed like time had slowed down, and I was completely disoriented. I couldn't feel anything – no scent, no sensation. It was just darkness, yet oddly, there was no pain. It was all so confusing that I passed out, sensing as if I were floating above myself, observing the chaos unfold below.

As my eyes fluttered open again, I found myself in a dimly lit hospital room surrounded by the constant beeping of machines and the hurried movements of medical personnel. The cacophony of voices and noise overwhelmed me, causing panic to set in as I struggled to piece together how I had arrived in this unfamiliar place. Flashes of a screeching car, blinding lights, and the horrifying sound of metal colliding rushed back to me, accompanied by waves of excruciating pain coursing through my body. It was then that I remembered - I had been in an accident.

The doctors requested that I maintain an upright posture during the X-ray procedure. Afterwards, they shared some startling information with me: my C2 and C3 vertebrae were fractured, and my spinal vertebrae were displaced. They referred to it as a "hangman's fracture". I discovered that this type of fracture earned its name because when these bones break, they exert pressure on the spinal cord, obstructing breathing and leading to immediate fatality. Interestingly, these are the very bones that break during hangings carried out as a form of capital punishment in our court processes.

Additionally, I was told that no one survives such a fracture, it is extremely rare. If someone does pull through, they often experience severe sensory loss, muscle weakness, and possibly paralysis, leading to a vegetative state.

Learning about the severity of my injury hit me like a ton of bricks. I was devastated. I was now in a lot of excruciating pain, both physical and emotional.

I remember the nurses and doctors poking my feet and limbs with sharp objects while I cried out in agony, only for them to stop abruptly. Despite the pain, I couldn't help but exclaim, "Ouch, that really hurts," which appeared to catch them off guard. Their faces reflected disbelief as they questioned me, "Are you absolutely certain?"

It was hard for them to comprehend when I mentioned that I could still feel sensations in my arms and legs. Luckily, my husband came out of the accident unscathed and was actually in better shape than I was.

The massive hospital we stayed at was managed by American physicians who offered subsidized medical services. Even though my injury was serious, I managed to improve. The doctor told me, " Young woman, you're resilient like a cat with nine lives. Very few survive such a catastrophic injury unscathed, and those who do are often left paralyzed. So go out there and embrace life; savor every moment." As I battled through the unbearable pain with the help of potent pain medication and the unwavering support of the hospital team, my days blurred into nights.

The accident completely changed my life. It was a lot to handle, from the initial shock to ongoing complications, medical care, and the need for personalized attention. My parents initially wanted to take me back to the village but realized they wouldn't be able to provide the care I needed to recover. As a result, I had to move in with my then-boyfriend, who later became my husband.

Throughout my medical treatment, I was required to don a massive metal brace that weighed a whopping fifty pounds for a period of four months. This brace played a vital role in ensuring that my neck stayed properly aligned. To my astonishment, the doctors had to resort to extreme measures by actually drilling into my forehead and skull to insert screws and bolts. Due to the sheer weight of the brace, I heavily relied on assistance for various activities like walking, sitting, lying down, and even personal hygiene. However, after the four-month mark, I was fortunate enough to switch to a more comfortable cervical brace, which I wore for an additional two months.

Despite being thankful for surviving the accident, the injury had a deep effect on me. It was so severe that I couldn't even remember my own name because of the brain trauma. I lost all my memories. Constructing simple sentences became difficult, and even recalling important details like my ID number, which I used to know effortlessly, felt impossible. The most frustrating part was having to begin from the beginning and relearn how to write and create meaningful sentences all over again.

Adding insult to injury, it was quite a struggle to handle the different needs we encountered every day. Simply put, everything seemed to come with a hefty price tag. Consequently, the most sensible course of action was to file a claim with our health insurance in order to have my medical expenses covered. My husband had the privilege of being covered by his employer's insurance, but unfortunately, I wasn't included in the policy. To rectify this, we had to show proof of our marriage or a committed relationship. As a result, we decided to sign a legal document called a "a promissory note" to formalize our relationship. However, this meant that I didn't get to experience a traditional white wedding ceremony, which was a bit disappointing.

For those who may not be familiar, let me explain what a promissory note is. It's basically a formal document that serves as proof that my husband and I, as grown adults, are living together as a married couple. Once we signed the promissory note, we made the decision to officially live together. And after three years of being together, we then went to the courthouse to legalize our marriage.

Just like that, in the blink of an eye, a severe injury - a hangman's fracture - had rendered me helpless. For four long months, I found myself confined to my back, trapped in a world of agony and immobility. The rigid brace shackled my movements, denying me the simple joys of sitting up or walking unaided.

The twins, full of innocence and unbounded love, embraced me as their own. Overnight, I had earned the title of "mother"! They would burst into my room each day, beaming smiles and fists full of dandelions. The girl twin, with her boundless energy and chatter, became my source of light in the darkness.

Despite his demanding work, my husband raced home every evening, ensuring my comfort and hygiene. A ray of hope in my dreary days, he stood by my side with unwavering devotion.

On the bright side, the years we spent together brought us closer, and we became best friends. My husband became my sole support system, showed me the world, and always pushed me to become a better version of myself. He helped me work on my studies, develop myself, and invest. Everything seemed to be falling into place; I went back to doing well in my studies and was happy with my husband, so eventually, we ended up having kids together.

However, it is important to note that there were certain warning signs that I overlooked because of my intense infatuation with him. He had deep-seated trust issues and displayed a significant amount of jealousy and control. For example, when cell phones first became available, I was completely oblivious to their inner workings. Little did I know, he had set up a system to forward all of my calls and messages to himself. It felt as though I was constantly being watched.

Later on, we ventured into the printing business, offering a range of products, including prepaid phone cards. I noticed a decline in our inventory, specifically the prepaid cards known as airtime back then. Despite questioning our employees and discussing the matter with my spouse, I could not make any headway. However, thanks to the unique serial numbers on the vouchers, I decided to dig deeper and uncovered the shocking truth - my beloved husband had been taking some of the vouchers without my knowledge or consent.

Afterwards, he cunningly falsified my signature in order to transfer all my properties and vehicles into his possession. Despite bringing the incident to the attention of the authorities, no headway was made. In due course, he went as far as depriving me of my academic certificates, transcripts, and passport just after I had secured an opportunity to study abroad. Although I was able to replace the passport, the loss of my transcripts and certificates was irreversible.

What a chaotic life! When love blinds you, it is easy to miss the red flags, just like I did. Despite encountering countless hurdles and manipulations, my determination to pursue my goals remained unwavering.

Another challenge that rocked our world was my inability to give my husband a male child, which is highly valued in many African cultures. Our relationship was now veiled in a cloud of ambiguity amidst cultural expectations.

The weight of having a son over a daughter had begun to bore down on us, the whispers of ancestors echoing in the wind, urging us to fulfill a duty as old as time itself. The pressure mounted a silent beast that prowled in the spaces between our words. Every smile had now become a hidden sorrow, every celebration shadowed by unspoken fears.

In numerous African cultures, the significance of having a son is greatly esteemed compared to having a daughter. This inclination towards boys is firmly embedded in tradition and remains widespread even in present times. Sons are regarded as the ultimate symbol of marital success. Parents aspire for a son to ensure the longevity of their union, placing immense expectations on partners to bear male offspring.

The weight of expectations can be overwhelming, particularly for men, since it determines the continuation of their family line. Those without a male heir may encounter judgment and exclusion from their society, causing the husband to feel as though he has no heritage to pass down. This could result in mockery and a feeling of inadequacy among his friends, leaving him feeling like a mere shadow of himself.

For more context, in African cultures, specific rituals are reserved for male children to perform after the passing of a man, adding to the preference for male offspring over female offspring.

In a society where the emphasis lies on men carrying forward the family lineage, some individuals have resorted to seeking companionship with other women to demonstrate their capability of fathering a son. It is understandable that wives would feel immense sorrow in such circumstances, leading to the unfortunate dissolution of their marriage.

In the midst of this scenario, while the world was in deep slumber, a crucial decision had to be made. My spouse had resorted to engaging in extramarital affairs. He had pursued relationships with our children's nannies, as well as some close friends and family members, all in an attempt to secure an heir or perhaps find himself a second wife. When I discovered this, I reached my breaking point. The weight of it all became unbearable. When I mustered the courage to confront him, he responded with physical aggression. The beating he inflicted upon me left me with a black eye and bruises scattered across my body. It was at that moment I realized I had to end this relationship. While forgiving infidelity was one thing, enduring physical abuse was an entirely different matter. I knew deep down that these beatings would never cease.

It was a stark truth that, despite my education and empowerment as a woman, societal expectations still loomed large. I was faced with the traditional choice of having a male child to carry on the family name or save my life. It felt like a suffocating weight on my shoulders, a burden that I struggled to shake off. In the midst of this turmoil, I found myself trapped in a never-ending cycle of domestic violence.

The man I once admired had become a mere shell of his former self. He was overtaken by rage and a need for control. I struggled to hide the bruises and emotional wounds, dreading the judgment and sympathy of those around me and society at large.

One day, I chose to walk away from the toxicity of my past. I realized that societal norms or expectations did not define my worth as a woman. I was more than just a vessel for bearing sons or a recipient of abuse. I was me and more, and as the sun set on the horizon, I knew that the future held endless possibilities for a woman who refused to be bound by tradition or fear. The unbroken.

I subsequently obtained a restraining order against him and initiated the divorce process. When I served him with the restraining order, the situation became much messier. He went as far as hiring a hitman to help him solve his problem quicker, to make me disappear forever.

There is this memorable incident that took place while I was enjoying some quality time with my colleagues at a bustling public spot. Out of the blue, two individuals approached our group, their eyes fixed on me intently. With a rather peculiar request, they uttered, "We've been observing you, and you strike us as a genuinely kind-hearted individual. Would you please pay us off?"

I was completely dumbfounded by that surprising encounter and immediately inquired about their true intentions. To my astonishment, they revealed that my husband had actually hired them to eliminate me, but now they had a change of heart and were willing to spare me if I paid them to call it off.

I asked for evidence, skeptical that someone could easily fabricate such a tale to scam me. They then presented me with a text message from my husband, ordering them to eliminate me during my commute home. The message conveyed a sense of urgency; the sinister plan had to be executed promptly.

At that point, I could feel myself losing control of my feet. I knew that it was not a bad dream. I had lived with that person for almost ten years and could see his number on the screen. This was extremely concerning, and I knew I had to report it to the police. However, this was not the first or last occasion. He made several attempts on my life, with one instance involving individuals he sent to follow me. Late one night, as I was heading home around 10 p.m., they pursued the car I was in and opened fire—truly a miraculous escape! Talk about having nine lives! By then, my life had gotten incredibly chaotic because of his actions.

The heartfelt plea from my father to reconsider my divorce and mend the broken relationship with him stemmed from genuine concern for my well-being. He was genuinely afraid that if I persisted on this path, my husband's possessiveness and anger might escalate to a point where the consequences could be dire, even fatal. Witnessing the anguish and defeat in my parents' eyes shattered my heart, but I couldn't find it within myself to return to a toxic environment that I knew would only bring harm.

Refusing to comply with my parents' wishes wasn't an act of defiance or a lack of respect; it was purely because I couldn't fathom the idea of sharing a roof with that individual ever again. However, as the saying goes, one should never say never. In due course, I experienced firsthand the extraordinary lengths to which love can stretch. While we all yearn for love and crave its presence, when it transforms into an all-consuming and malevolent force, it has the power to inflict unimaginable anguish and drive one to the brink of insanity. It took me a while to fully comprehend the depths of his capabilities, and by then, the situation had already spiraled out of control.

I did, however, conquer this issue because I had confidence that I would. Despite the unfortunate turn of events and attempts to finish me, I kept the faith and excelled in my endeavors and career. In Kenya, I worked as a veterinarian while continuing my education for a year in the Netherlands. Inspired by my father's commitment to the profession, I found my true calling in veterinary medicine after accompanying him on his visits to farms.

So, I studied hard in school and was admitted into the greatest veterinary school in the country. The curriculum required us to succeed in academics and clinical skills, which did not seem like a challenge because I understood it was all part of getting to my destination.

All of it was in the chart of my life from the very beginning. In the grand scheme of things, veterinary school proved to be quite challenging. It required countless hours of studying, back-to-back classes, and pulling all-nighters to go through the material with minimal time for rest before taking the exams. Throughout this period, I experimented with various strategies to stay alert through the night in order to get ready for my tests.

For example, my friends and I had some unconventional methods to keep ourselves awake during those long nights. We would dip our feet into freezing buckets of water or gulp down countless cups of coffee. Let me tell you, studying in that place was no piece of cake. It demanded sheer dedication and an unwavering commitment to hard work.

It took me six long years of dedication and perseverance, but I can proudly announce that I successfully obtained my veterinary medicine degree. This accomplishment not only brought me immense joy but also filled my family, particularly my father, with overwhelming happiness. Witnessing their beaming smiles on the day of my graduation made every ounce of hard work completely worthwhile.

As I walked across the stage on my graduation day, I found myself wearing two hats, little did I know that as I was reciting the veterinarian oath, I was also beginning to experience the early stages of labor. November 4th, 2002, became a day of double celebration for me, not only did I receive my veterinary degree, but I also welcomed my daughter Elsa Yvette into the world. What was meant to be a simple graduation ceremony turned into a momentous occasion, marking the start of a new chapter in my life.

Throughout my journey as a parent, I've lovingly referred to my children as my "academic babies," a term they have wholeheartedly embraced, showcasing their exceptional academic prowess. It's truly remarkable to witness their individual achievements in the realm of education. As fate would have it, my daughter Elna graced our lives shortly after I triumphed over my postgraduate exams, while Hadasha, our youngest bundle of joy, entered the world during my relentless pursuit of a Ph.D. in the Netherlands.

My passion for learning and reading has always been evident, but my dedication to excelling in my career as a veterinarian was equally strong. I was certain that, with time, I would gain invaluable experience in the field. Starting with routine tasks like deworming, giving vaccinations, and nail trimming, I honed my skills until I faced my first complex case: Simba, a German shepherd injured in a car crash. The memory of that particular incident remains vivid in my thoughts.

Simba had darted in front of a moving vehicle. The accident had left Simba with severe injuries to his pelvic bones and rear feet beyond repair. It was heartbreaking to have to euthanize him.

Throughout my career, I have had the privilege of conducting a wide range of surgeries and procedures. From intricate dental work and successful tumor removals to the delicate art of setting bones and even performing life-saving cesarean sections, I have witnessed the incredible impact these interventions can have on people's lives. Despite the obstacles and difficulties that come with each case, I can confidently say that every single experience has been immensely rewarding. The satisfaction of knowing that I have made a positive difference in someone's life is priceless, and I wouldn't exchange these moments for anything in the world.

My patients were of great value to me and deserved the utmost medical attention possible. In addition to gaining practical knowledge, there was also the opportunity to interact with pet owners and understand their perspectives. Occasionally, the information provided by the owners did not match what I observed in the patient, requiring me to delve deeper. Throughout my career, I have noticed that individuals tend to be selective in sharing information with doctors, necessitating the need to piece together the puzzle in order to formulate an effective treatment plan.

When I first began working in my field, I quickly realized that pet owners would often leave out important details about their animals, thinking certain behaviors or health issues were embarrassing or reflected poorly on them as caretakers. An owner might mention that their dog was timid but not disclose that the dog had severe separation anxiety that led to destructive chewing behaviors anytime he was left alone. Or a cat owner would talk about how their pet threw up occasionally but not reveal that the cat was throwing up multiple times a week, likely due to an undiagnosed chronic illness. As caretakers, we had to learn to ask the right probing questions and build trust with owners to get the full picture in order to diagnose and support the animals properly.

This communication gap inspired me to start an animal welfare movement aimed at educating pet owners. We held seminars and produced brochures to teach owners how to monitor their pets' health, recognize symptoms that warranted a vet visit, provide enrichment to avoid problem behaviors, and have open conversations with their veterinarian. I found that most owners wanted to do right for their pets but simply lacked the knowledge of how to best care for them. By giving owners, the information and resources they needed while also creating a judgment-free space for them to ask questions and raise concerns, we empowered them to become better caretakers. The animal welfare movement led to pets receiving higher quality care and owners feeling more confident and fulfilled in their roles. I was so proud to be a part of driving that positive change.

Prior to the painful breakup, my spouse had been an unwavering pillar of support, recognizing abilities within me that I had failed to acknowledge. Continuously, he urged me to aim higher and utilize my veterinary expertise to bring about tangible change. His unwavering faith in my capabilities propelled me to venture beyond my familiar boundaries and embrace fresh professional prospects, despite the gradual decline of our bond.

Even though our marriage came to a difficult end, I will forever be grateful for his encouragement in those formative years. His belief in my abilities inspired me to step out of my comfort zone and pursue a thrilling opportunity at the government's Veterinary Vaccine Research Institute. This role aligned perfectly with my skills and enabled me to make the most of my veterinary background. Working as a researcher at the Institute, I spearheaded projects focused on studying diseases in livestock and creating vaccines to safeguard both the animals and our food sources. My responsibilities included conducting lab experiments and engaging in partnerships with fellow scientists and stakeholders.

I found the work incredibly rewarding, knowing my efforts could have a real impact on animal health and agricultural production nationwide. On top of the research, I was also able to share my knowledge through training programs for veterinary students and livestock producers. Teaching the next generation of vets and collaborating directly with farmers to implement disease prevention measures were extremely fulfilling parts of the role.

It was a gratifying experience to realize that our endeavors were making a significant impact in safeguarding the lives of animals. We disseminated vaccines and medical care, gathered samples, and thoroughly examination of facilities, as well as the visits to various project sites. Occasionally, the work required us to travel to distant areas with extreme weather conditions, but it was all worth it in the end.

Balancing work and family life was a constant challenge for me, often keeping me away from my loved ones for weeks at a time. However, it worked out for me because I could afford to have two nannies—one for looking after the kids and the other for handling the household chores—which made things a bit easier. Plus, working for the government makes it easier for you to have necessities provided by your employer, like being chauffeured from home to work and vice versa, affordable housing, and big yards to grow organic vegetables and fruits, raise your backyard chickens, or even keep dairy goats!

Both my marriage and professional experiences have played crucial roles in shaping my life. These two facets have significantly influenced all aspects of my life and have played a part in molding me into the individual I am today. I felt it was essential to incorporate them into my book to convey to readers that it is possible to seize control of your life and evolve positively even after facing challenges.

Chapter 3: Coming To America

I NEVER THOUGHT MY LIFE would take me on a journey driven by faith, but it has. Growing up, In the quiet hours of the evening, as the sun dipped below the horizon and the stars began to twinkle in the darkening sky, I often found myself contemplating the mysteries of life and the endless possibilities. I was not sure if the belief that had been instilled in me came from my parents or some other ethereal source. It felt as though I had absorbed it through the very air I breathed, like a whisper in the wind that lingered in the depths of my soul. It is like that feeling you get after attending a personal growth seminar themed "You are what you think."

From an early age, as I gazed up at the airplanes crisscrossing the sky, their lights blinking in the darkness like celestial messengers, I felt a sense of boundless possibility within me.

For so many, the American dream was the ultimate symbol of hope and opportunity. But for me, it was something more elusive, more intangible.

It was the belief that my life was meant for greatness, that my journey was just beginning, an adventure waiting to unfold. And so, as I stood beneath the vast expanse of the night sky, I knew one thing for certain - my story was just beginning, and it was up to me to write the next chapter.

When I arrived in this country more than ten years ago, I had no clue about the challenges that awaited me as I pursued my dreams. Despite facing unexpected obstacles and setbacks, I managed to achieve several small victories that eventually led to bigger successes. Reflecting on those years now feels like strolling down a red carpet.

Moving to a new country with a family is both exciting and daunting. The sense of uncertainty that overwhelmed us upon our arrival in the United States remains vivid in my memory. The real struggle began when we realized we had no way to communicate in this unfamiliar territory. Without a US phone number to seek assistance, we felt lost in a sea of unfamiliarity. To make matters worse, our baby's urgent need for milk only heightened the anxiety of an already difficult situation.

As we landed in the United States, excitement fizzed through our veins, but a cold grip of worry danced in our hearts. The plan was to stay with a host that had vanished into thin air, leaving us stranded at the airport.

The towering skyscrapers and honking yellow cabs painted a vibrant backdrop to our journey. Each step was tinged with both awe and apprehension. Our children's wide eyes, excitement, and eager chatter put a smile on our faces as we tried to mask the underlying uncertainty. Our family of five, laden with suitcases and a month-old infant, coursed through the airport into the "Big Apple State."

I remember as our departure date to the US drew closer, our efforts to reach out to our host proved futile. Despite the looming uncertainty, we refused to let panic cloud our judgment. We knew panic would not be our ally. Instead, we donned the metaphorical cap of faith and boarded the plane at Jomo Kenyatta International Airport (JKIA) in Kenya, bound for JFK, New York, on a one-way ticket.

Touching down at JFK on a chilly December 26, 2013, amidst a flurry of snow, we found ourselves engulfed in a wave of emotions. Armed with five bulging suitcases and our three children, we stood in awe, unsure of what awaited us in this foreign land. The bitter cold embraced us, casting a shadow of doubt over our next move. Uncertain of our next steps, we phoned friends in Kenya who provided names of nearby hotels – notably, La Quinta by Wyndham. However, securing a cab to take us there proved more challenging than we had anticipated. We found a taxi, and the driver, with a wide smile, ushered us into the yellow cab. Little did we know, we were in for an unexpected detour.

The driver, sensing our unfamiliarity with the city, took a circuitous route, making perplexing turns that seemed to lead us further away from our destination. With each mile, our unease grew. Suddenly, he veered off the main road and onto an expressway, claiming it was to avoid traffic. But our suspicion heightened when he began to muse about the beautiful sights this detour offered while pointing out toll signs.

Thirty miles later, the cab finally ground to a halt in front of our hotel. The moment of reckoning arrived when the driver casually announced the fare - an exorbitant USD 250, insisting we were responsible for the extra tolls! Shock and disbelief washed over us - the journey was meant to be just a few miles, not a scenic tour around the city. Despite this setback, we simply wished him well. Thankfully, we were grateful he reached the destination, preventing us from being stranded at the JFK gates.

We stayed at the hotel for three days, unsure of our next move until necessity pushed us to action. Our attempts to seek assistance from the Kenyan community on social media were met with impractical and extreme suggestions that left us bewildered, some impractical or too extreme that I cannot recount them here.

Amid the turmoil, a glimmer of hope appeared in the form of a heavenly woman who generously offered her friend's residence as a safe haven for us. "Stay until you regain your independence or find a place to call your own," Cathy expressed to us. Her words provided comfort to our troubled souls. Daphne and Catherine truly came through for us. Their compassion knew no bounds. They paved the way for us to find solace in the warm embrace of another family who treated us as their own. Rosemary has been the epitome of an aunt that anyone could hope for. Alongside her family, they have been the backbone of support for my own family. And then there is Londa - a sister to me, despite not being related by blood - who told me, "Listen, your daughters are my own." What an incredible blessing!

The journey to settle down was paved with paperwork and occasional fees, but with the unwavering support of our newfound community, we overcame each obstacle. In just four months, we were able to move into our own humble home.

It all began when I submitted an application for a green card to the United States in 2016, only to unintentionally forget about it. For over five years, my partner had been trying without success to secure a visa, exploring options in the USA, Canada, Australia, and various other countries. During our marriage, I took a chance to obtain a green card with my partner. Unfortunately, a couple of years down the line, our marriage came to an end, resulting in our parting ways, getting divorced, and embarking on academic pursuits in the Netherlands. Amidst the windmills and tulip fields of the Netherlands where I was living, I was pleasantly surprised to find out that I had won the green card lottery! It was truly unexpected and exciting. Let's just consider that every choice has a consequence.

Allow me to take you back in time, just a year before all of this happened. I found myself at a crossroads where I had to make a crucial decision that would shape the future of my family. With the responsibility of being the sole breadwinner, I knew that pursuing my education in the Netherlands was the key to unlocking a brighter future for us all. It was a daunting choice, but one that I knew deep down was necessary for the betterment of our lives.

As I observed my young family from a distance, the gravity of my choice would weigh heavily on my shoulders. I bore the sole responsibility of caring for my children and had entrusted their well-being to a nanny and my brother in Kenya. However, there were moments when intense waves of emotion would hit me, leaving me feeling overwhelmed and vulnerable.

A trusted friend became a lifeline, bridging the gap that separated me from my beloved children. Like a watchful guardian, she skillfully managed the household affairs, diligently handling the finances and ensuring the nanny received compensation on time. Alas! This fragile arrangement was shattered when my husband, without my knowledge or consent, took matters into his own hands, relocating our children to his ancestral village.

Upon receiving the photos from him, I was confronted with a solemn scene. In the snapshots, I could discern the shadows of sadness in my children's eyes, a stark contrast to the lively laughter I remembered. The ache in my heart grew deeper as I heard accounts of hardship and neglect through phone calls and messages.

The darkest moment arrived during a tearful conversation with my nine-year-old daughter. Her innocent voice trembled as she relayed the harsh reality they faced - meals of mere scraps and hunger gnawing at their little stomachs. Each word she uttered felt like a stab in my soul, a reminder of the price I unwillingly made them pay for my aspirations.

They were told that certain foods, such as meat and chicken, were reserved for elders or visitors, relegating them to a diet of greens and grains on their plates.

Then, one day, my daughter, with a troubled voice, revealed a darker secret. She disclosed how an older cousin, nearly a man, had crossed the line with her, making her uncomfortable and fearful. He had made inappropriate advances toward her. My heart sank at her words, rage bubbling beneath the surface.

Furious and shaken, I wasted no time in contacting my husband, who shared my concern. He assured me he would address the issue with the distant cousin, but deep down, I knew that mere words might not be enough to protect our children from harm.

He relocated them to an obscure rental property that I found unsatisfactory. When the opportunity arose, I flew back to Kenya with a single goal: to rescue my children. I knew this would not be without conflict with my husband.

I shared my intentions with my father, hoping for his support, but he strongly advised against it. Owing to the patriarchal norms of our society, children were traditionally seen as belonging to the man. However, I could not accept his counsel. My brother and I devised a plan. The morning after my husband left for work, I collected my children and made our escape. My brother drove us to the bus stop as if every second counted, and we returned to Nairobi.

Returning to the Netherlands, I had to leave my children behind once more. This time, however, I ensured that I had a court order served to him, establishing that I had full custody while the divorce case was still being resolved in court. My scholarship was modest; I could not afford to have my children join me. I solemnly promised my children that, before long, I would find a way to bring them with me. Talk about the power of positive thinking!

I was overjoyed to discover that I had won the US green card! I hadn't checked the website for some time, and the expiration date was rapidly approaching. The lengthy process of handling paperwork, attending visa interviews, and accomplishing other tasks was beginning to put pressure on me.

In order to meet the deadline, I took the initiative to apply for my visa as the main applicant at the US embassy in the Netherlands. I then arranged appointments for my family back in Nairobi. Being pregnant at the time, I sought help from my husband, who was listed as a beneficiary on my application.

Understanding the importance of our children's future, we made the decision to relocate to America as a family, despite the challenges in our relationship.

The age-old saying, "A leopard can't change its spots," rang true once again. Despite his facade of seeking reconciliation, his true intentions were solely focused on himself. As soon as we arrived, he swiftly took back his possessions and acted as if we were strangers. His actions clearly showed that his priority was himself, leaving me feeling used, ignored, and mistreated.

After settling down in the United States for only six months, I unexpectedly had to return to Kenya to gather the necessary data for my Ph.D. research. Little did I know that during my stay in the rural villages of Kenya, my husband started monitoring my movements once again, with the malicious intention of causing harm. To ensure my safety, I had to adopt a cat-and-mouse strategy, constantly staying one step ahead of him. At that point, he had already circulated gossip extensively, claiming that he was the rightful recipient of the green card and insinuating that he had only invited me because I happened to be the mother of his children. He dropped subtle hints that he might be having second thoughts about his choice.

After a span of approximately four months, I found myself back in the United States. The atmosphere at home with my husband had turned into a delicate and demanding situation, where I had to tread carefully, as if walking on fragile eggshells. Throughout this difficult experience, I patiently waited for the right moment to navigate through the ordeal.

In April 2015, a year and a half since our relocation to the United States, the situation had become incredibly difficult. Our relationship had deteriorated to the point where we felt like complete strangers, and it appeared that there was no way to mend the broken pieces. It was then that I discovered his plans to visit Kenya, as he had a son there whom he had never met before. Juggling our busy schedules was no easy feat - with him working during the day and me taking the night shift from 11 pm to 7 am to accommodate our children. On top of that, I was also pursuing a master's degree at Rutgers University in New Jersey, adding another layer of chaos to our already hectic lives.

As I was getting ready for another day at work, my phone rang unexpectedly. It was my daughter calling me late in the evening, just before 11 pm. Her voice sounded urgent as she informed me about an unexpected turn of events. "Dad is frantically packing his belongings and there are police officers present," she exclaimed. The news caught me off guard, and I couldn't help but wonder what had transpired in the hours leading up to this moment.

This revelation left me stunned and bewildered. I was in absolute shock. Like, what? I tried calling him, but I was blocked. As I tried to process what had happened, nothing made sense! After dialing 911, I connected with the station and conversed with the officers who had recently visited our residence. With a mix of shock and disbelief, I questioned them, "Why on earth would you allow him to leave young children unsupervised and unattended?" They relayed a story that contradicted what I knew. According to them, "He had stated that he needed an escort to maintain peace while he picked up his things, claiming you would not allow him."

In relation to the kids, they mentioned, "He made a false statement about your working hours, saying that you were employed from 3 pm to 11 pm and would arrive home shortly after he departed."

It was a stressful night. I asked the police officer to keep an eye on my kids while I sought a replacement at work. I reached my house at 1 am, driving like crazy through the night.

"We were just on the verge of contacting the Children's Protective Services," the officers disclosed, "since it wasn't within our duties to act as babysitters."

My anger surged through me like a raging storm. With a fiery glare, I snapped back, "You should have ensured the accuracy of the facts before pointing fingers at me!"

It was quite a hectic time, so I decided to take a break from work for a week to sort out my routine. You know what they say? karma has a way of catching up, and justice can sometimes be swift! My husband was in such a rush to escape and secretly head to Kenya that he ended up in a bit of a pickle - he either lost or forgot his passport! As a result, his travel plans were thwarted. A few days later, he came back, expressing regret and seeking another opportunity to co-parent our kids. Can you believe it? What would you do if you were In my position?

Ever since he had suddenly left, my daughters had been deeply affected. They insisted on sleeping with the lights on, but even that couldn't ease their fears. We tried double-bolting the doors and barricading them with furniture, but it was all in vain.

Since the rental agreement was in his name, I knew I had to find a new place to live. I had reached my breaking point. Thankfully, one positive aspect of the US system is that you receive a tax return after filing your taxes, which was a small silver lining in my modest income. I wisely used that money to cover the deposit, two months' rent, and purchase some essential household items. Finally, in May of 2015, we were able to move out and start afresh.

During that time, my daughters provided immense emotional support, constantly cheering us on and reassuring me that things would turn out fine. I am truly grateful for having such an amazing support system. The relocation went smoothly, and fortunately, switching schools didn't impact my daughters' academic performance. A year later, we relocated to a nicer home, and within three years, we were able to purchase our own place.

Breaking free from a relationship can be quite a daunting task, particularly when the other person's desire to reconcile is not entirely sincere. "Let's do it for the sake of our children" may seem like a compelling reason to agree, but it can actually be a perilous path to tread. It requires immense courage and inner strength to continue forging ahead. Despite the initial obstacles, releasing a grip on the past often proves to be the wisest decision, as it paves the way for both individuals to discover their own happiness.

As soon as we settled into our new place and reality sank in, my husband started persistently urging us to reconcile. However, was completely over it by then. There was no part of me that wanted to go back. It's unbelievable, just two weeks later, after bombarding us with endless messages and facing our firm rejections, he shockingly reported us as missing! I was absolutely dumbfounded. What in the world was he thinking?

Out of the blue, I got a call from the FBI regarding a peculiar claim that I had gone missing. Interestingly enough, they had already reached out to my workplace, but luckily for me, I had taken the day off.

Perplexed, I couldn't help but question the caller, "If you're talking to me right now, how can I possibly be missing?"

In order to resolve any confusion, I made my way to the closest police station and provided them with our text conversation as evidence of our communication. This clearly demonstrated that he was aware of our decision to move out, leaving no doubt that we were not missing. At this point, I also went ahead and petitioned for full custody of my children.

I contacted my lawyer in Kenya to expedite my divorce case. Little did I know, my divorce had already been granted by the judge in Kenya before we even set foot in the US. I was delighted when my lawyer informed me about this, as it meant that my husband had no legal claim to my green card. I immediately thanked my lawyer for speeding up the process and ensuring my freedom.

Over the course of three years, my husband successfully brought one of his numerous girlfriends, who happened to be a nanny for our children, into the United States. Without my knowledge, he divorced me in the US, married the nanny, believing it would deeply wound me.

Rumors had been circulating about a wedding taking place at one of my husband's friend's residences here in Jersey. A group of relatives from Kenya was scheduled to fly in for the occasion. Interestingly, one of the members of this entourage was a girl who had initially arrived on a visitor's visa but had managed to stay and even change her status to 'Mrs.' It wasn't something that bothered me at the moment, but my husband seemed to have a different perspective on the matter.

My husband is always convinced he's the one in charge and a brilliant strategist. He was determined to enjoy all the privileges of U.S. citizenship, such as voting, serving on a jury, and getting a U.S. passport. Having been a green card holder in the U.S. for the mandatory five years, he made up his mind to pursue citizenship. Believing he could outwit the process, he attended the citizenship interview solo, even though our family had immigrated together years ago.

It was quite a spectacle when he was asked about his family of five. He boldly insisted that he had gone through a divorce and even presented a dubious divorce certificate as proof. These sketchy divorce services shamelessly advertise on billboards, luring people with promises of ending marriages without any complications involving their partners. Nevertheless, I suspect that immigration authorities were already aware of our legitimate divorce in Kenya, either through official records or through rumors circulating around.

It didn't take long for his deceitful ways to catch up with him, ultimately leading to the rejection of his citizenship application. It's evident that my husband's insatiable desire for things blinded him to the thorough scrutiny he would face. Instead of ensuring his place in this country, his cunning tactics only hindered his journey towards becoming a citizen.

As I pen down these words and conclude this chapter, it dawns on me that this might be my chance to sever all connections with him, vowing never to speak of him again in the days to come. However, it is crucial to bear in mind that individuals cross our paths for a purpose. They either bring blessings or impart valuable lessons. Regardless of the duration of their presence, be it a fleeting moment or a lifelong companionship, we ought to embrace their existence and gracefully move forward once we grasp their significance in our journey.

Chapter 4: The American Dream

THE AMERICAN DREAM has always been a powerful symbol of hope and opportunity in the United States. It promotes the idea that anyone can achieve success and prosperity, no matter where they come from. I was captivated by the idea of this Dream - the notion that hard work and perseverance could lead to boundless opportunities and success in the land of freedom and possibility. Growing up in a foreign country, this dream seemed like a distant fantasy, but it only fueled my ambitions, and inspired me to set sail for a brighter future. Little did I know that one day, it would become my reality. In this chapter, I want to take you along on my journey to building a successful life in America, facing the challenges that came with it, and achieving my version of the American Dream.

Before I embark on my story, it is essential to grasp the core essence of the American Dream. Although its meaning has transformed over the years, the enduring belief that hard work and determination can lead to a better life remains unwavering. This ageless symbol of hope and possibility continues to ignite the spirits of countless American generations, compelling them to pursue their dreams and create a meaningful impact on society.

My journey towards the American Dream began with a significant decision - saying goodbye to my native land in pursuit of a better tomorrow in the United States. Just like many other immigrants, my voyage was filled with numerous challenges and obstacles. Nevertheless, with a strong determination and faith in a greater force, I overcame these difficulties and started to lay a strong foundation for both my family and self.

Not everyone realizes the challenges that immigrants encounter when seeking employment in a new country. Language barriers, visa limitations, and cultural differences can all pose significant obstacles. Fortunately, my green card allowed me to navigate the job market more easily. I started with a part-time job earning $11 per hour, juggling work responsibilities with parenting duties. With hard work and determination, I worked my way up from an assistant manager to a manager, earning higher wages at each promotion.

In the midst of all that was going on, I couldn't help but face the harsh reality of owning a car in the U.S., especially when comparing it to my experience in the Netherlands where having a car was seen as more of a luxury rather than a necessity. However, as I started to establish myself here, the significance of having a reliable mode of transportation became crystal clear. Determined to find an affordable option, I tirelessly scoured through Craigslist, hoping to stumble upon a suitable choice. Eventually, my search led me to a green Subaru Impreza, an older model, which I purchased for $1600 in cash from Brooklyn, New York. Unfortunately, this acquisition took a considerable chunk out of my savings.

The aging car's worn leather interior and sporadic stalling suggested its years on the road, yet it was a good beginning. Unfortunately, after only 10 miles into our trip, the radiator started acting up, billowing steam. Our impromptu pit stops for cooling down on the side of the road soon became a regular occurrence, much to the amusement of onlookers. A trip to the mechanic uncovered a long list of problems, all needing expensive repairs that we couldn't afford. Undeterred, I soldiered on, using the vehicle to work until it finally surrendered, sputtering its last breath on a particularly unforgiving Monday morning.

Growing up in Kenya, my first reaction was to reach for a jug of water and address the overheating engine just like I used to do in my homeland. Little did I know, a kind stranger would educate me on the dangers of frozen radiator tubes and the magic of antifreeze, revealing the extent of my automotive naivety.

A Kenyan family extended a generous offer to purchase this vehicle for a mere $300, assuring that they would eventually settle the payment. But alas, their promise vanished into thin air, just like mist dissipating under the morning sun, leaving the vehicle deserted on the vibrant streets of the bustling township. As if destiny had a wicked sense of humor, parking tickets mysteriously found their way to my mailbox.

My gut feeling warned me that this family wouldn't follow through with the deal. Despite my many efforts to get back the vehicle, they eventually insisted that I cough up $150 for a new battery they said they had put in. With a heavy heart, I handed over the money, only to discover that the car was beyond repair. In the end, I decided to sell the clunker for $150, putting an end to a regrettable investment.

Amidst the chaos and disappointments, there was one constant—I refused to let these events define my path. With an unwavering resolve as my compass, I traded wheels for rails and embraced the bustling cityscape as I walked the reminder of the miles to and from work. As night descended, a new set of challenges emerged. The dimly lit streets took on an eerie ambiance, with shadows whimsically dancing in the ever-changing weather patterns. However, amidst the uncertainty, I unearthed a wellspring of inner strength, fueled by my unwavering perseverance. The obstacles I faced only served to fuel my determination to push forward.

When it was time to buy my second car, I found myself standing on the threshold of hope at a used car dealership. With no credit history backing me, my only companion was relentless optimism. I handed the dealer my modest pay stubs, displaying a weekly income of a mere $500. His eyes lingered on the numbers, contemplating my financial situation.

In an unexpected turn of events, the dealer proposed a sleek car priced at $8500 – a figure that seemed astronomical in my reality. I could not fathom locking away my hard-earned money for three years to afford that luxury. Instead, I opted for a more seasoned vehicle, cheaper but plagued with its own set of challenges.

The overused automobile did not pass the Motor Vehicle inspection just once or twice, but a whopping three times. It also had a knack for leaving me stranded on the side of the road, forcing me to shell out a fortune for a tow truck. Yet, despite all its imperfections, that car stood by my side through thick and thin. It became a loyal companion, symbolizing resilience In times of struggle.

Eventually, I found myself driving a magnificent $25,000 car, complete with all the bells and whistles. I put down a $5,000 down payment. Looking back on my journey, I am amazed by how far I have come. The road was rough, with unexpected turns and setbacks, but it brought me to a point where I could confidently choose any vehicle with certainty. Yet, amidst the glamour of success, I realize that priorities evolve with time.

The American dream, once a distant mirage, now stands within arm's reach. I've learned that perseverance and unwavering determination can pave the way to a reality where dreams are not just imagined but lived. In the rearview mirror of life, I see a testament to the truth that resilience conquers all obstacles on the road to success.

Yet, as my family navigated through the challenges, my two eldest daughters, who were 11 and 9 years old back then, became my unwavering support and pillars of strength. We formed an inseparable bond, fueled by love and unwavering determination. Despite their tender age, they took on responsibilities that exceeded their years, taking care of their younger sibling and assisting with household tasks. They had to grow up quickly. I would say matured at an accelerated pace, and decision-making became a collective effort - where their viewpoints held equal importance to mine.

I have to admit that there were both great days and not-so-great days. Even during the tough times, I made sure to keep a smile on my face for my loved ones. They were my driving force to push myself and give my all. My goal was to provide us with a good life full of opportunities and teach them the importance of hard work and honesty. To this day, financial literacy has remained a big topic at our dinner table.

Sundays hold a special place in our hearts. It is a day of spiritual nourishment at church, followed by blissful relaxation, reconnecting with friends, or indulging in a captivating movie. Our circle of friends mostly comprises fellow immigrants, just like us. These precious moments are priceless, irreplaceable. Within our immigrant community, we foster an unbreakable bond of sisterhood and brotherhood. We exchange tales of hope and inspiration, share newfound opportunities, offer guidance, and uplift one another through heartfelt prayers.

In our early days, we gathered for worship in the heart of New York City, specifically in the vibrant borough of the Bronx. It was a remarkable experience to immerse we in the bustling city atmosphere and relish the exquisite flavors of African delicacies served in its diverse eateries. However, as our path led us further south, we stumbled upon a new sanctuary where we could continue our spiritual journey and find solace.

In 2018, I made a phone call to wish a member of my congregation in New York a Happy New Year. It had been almost two years since we last spoke. Unfortunately, the conversation took an unexpected turn. The person on the other end hesitated, claiming to be unaware of my identity. After politely reintroducing myself, my fellow congregant seemed utterly astonished.

To my surprise, she blurted out, "I thought you had returned to Africa."

Confused, I asked, "Why would you think that?"

Her response caught me off guard as she said, "I simply assumed you had given up and left for Africa."

She must have "missed the memo." Nevertheless, this interaction was a clear indication of how situations may seem grim when viewed from an external point of view. Yet, even during the most challenging times, optimism and determination can lead us towards a brighter path. There is always a ray of hope shining at the end of the tunnel.

While I was successful in my first job, I realized I had more to offer and wanted to break into corporate America. With that objective in mind, I obtained a master's degree at Rutgers University, which significantly expanded my abilities and knowledge in my chosen sector. This extra knowledge helped me get my first corporate job in 2017 with a competitive wage.

However, I hit a bump in the road when my role was eliminated during a corporate restructuring, I didn't let it deter me. Instead, I pushed forward and quickly landed a new contract role that offered similar compensation. Over time, I achieved my ultimate goal of becoming a Drug Safety Veterinarian, enjoying a generous six-figure salary, incredible benefits, and a well-deserved retirement package.

As I ascended the ladder of success in my professional journey, a multitude of opportunities presented themselves to us. The attainment of financial stability became an integral part of my vision of the American Dream. A solid financial base not only enables us to chase grander aspirations but also allows us to craft a life of comfort and relish the rewards of our hard work. The transition from being tenants to proud homeowners in a delightful community marked a momentous achievement in our quest for happiness. With our financial footing firmly established, we eagerly seized the opportunity to indulge in the delights of exploration and travel, cherishing the fruits of our labor along the way.

We were captivated by the magical enchantment of Disney World, the sun-kissed beaches of Myrtle Beach, and the exotic allure of Puerto Rico. Our thirst for adventure led us to explore captivating destinations around the world. From the golden sands of Cancun and the serene beauty of Tulum in Mexico to the awe-inspiring wonders of Greece and the irresistible charm of the United Kingdom, our lives were filled with endless exploration. With each journey, we not only accumulated sky miles but also cherished priceless memories that would last a lifetime.

As I embarked on thrilling escapades, I always kept in mind the importance of financial education. Making sure my daughters understood the ins and outs of money management became a priority for me. I made sure they understood how technology can be a powerful tool for saving. I taught them the significance of being prepared for unforeseen expenses. Empowering them with tech applications like Acorns for saving and educating them about investment fundamentals through platforms like Robinhood and the stock market. This has truly been a game-changer for us.

Camping trips brought our family closer together, igniting a passion for adventure. This led us to purchase an RV, representing the newfound freedom and adaptability that came with our improved financial situation.

As we embarked on each expedition, whether metaphorically or literally, around the world, we realized that genuine wealth isn't just discovered in the locations we visit but also in the knowledge we exchange and the unforgettable moments we create.

Achieving the American Dream is still within reach in today's world. Yet, through my own journey, I've come to realize that success is not a walk in the park. It demands unwavering determination and a humble attitude to learn from those who have already tasted triumph. Keep your spirits high and push forward, even when faced with countless hurdles. Success is not a gift on a silver platter; it demands your unwavering commitment, the willingness to make sacrifices, and an unshakeable belief in yourself.

If you need an extra push, just think about this: I came to America with just five suitcases, three kids, and a dream. No family or friends, but I was determined to make a new life. Through hard work and perseverance, I made it happen. I'm living proof that with dedication, the American Dream is within reach.

Allow me to share a disclaimer before we proceed. Throughout my journey, I have honed my methods, discovering the need to "work smarter, not harder". Every obstacle has become a steppingstone, and every setback has revealed valuable lessons. I have remained steadfast in pursuing my aspirations. Today, as I gaze upon the horizon of possibilities, I see not just a house bought with sweat and sacrifice but a future brimming with endless possibilities. The harmonious tune of triumph continues to resound through my Real Estate ventures and Entrepreneurial pursuits, – the symphony of success plays on, its melody a testament to the undying spirit of a dreamer who dared to defy the odds.

Henry Ford's powerful message continues to inspire me, echoing through my mind each day: "Whether you think you can, or you think you can't--you're right." As I navigate through challenges and changes, my determination remains unwavering, a reminder of the resilience needed for whatever we pursue in life. While my path might have been different from others, the outcome has been the same—a life rich with endless opportunities and success.

Chapter 5: Finding Love Again

THE IDEA OF REDISCOVERING love can be intimidating, especially after experiencing heartbreak or the end of a long-term relationship. Opening up to someone new may seem like an impossible task. However, it could also be a silver lining, or the start of a new chapter filled with endless opportunities. To me, it would represent a new dawn, a chance to reset, to bid farewell to the past, and to simply savor the moment.

The day I met my partner was just a regular day at work, the kind that blended seamlessly from one hour to the next without any hint of magic in the air I can still picture the entrance of this man into the room bright and early. He greeted everyone in a casual manner, not directing his words to anyone specific, yet my coworker chimed in as they were acquainted.

s I observed him standing there, towering and strikingly good-looking, an air of self-assurance surrounded him. Strangely enough, this aura instantly triggered a sense of aversion within me. When he introduced himself as a maintenance worker, I simply replied with an indifferent "alright." If there was any flicker of attraction in that moment, it was overshadowed by my disdain for his overwhelming confidence, which felt more daunting than alluring.

We bumped into each other a few more times down the line. Although I initially found him a tad arrogant, my perception of him didn't waver. He claims he tried to greet me, but he thinks I just casually dismissed his "hellos".

Amidst the challenges of finding a new place to live and healing from a difficult breakup, I found myself needing to purchase household items that required heavy lifting and rearranging. Eager to address this dilemma, I asked a coworker,

"Hey, do you happen to know where I can rent a moving truck? Or maybe you know someone who could lend a hand with my move?"

Without missing a moment, she responded, "You should definitely reach out to Ron, the maintenance guy. He's got a truck that could do the trick!"

A deep sigh escaped my lips, carrying with it the weight of the impending conversation. The thought of reconnecting with him, someone I had deliberately kept at arm's length, sent shivers down my spine. But despite my reservations, I swallowed my pride and found the strength to reach out. "Hey, do you think you could help me out with moving a few things?" I asked tentatively.

He didn't waste a second before responding, "Absolutely. Just let me know when you're ready." I reassured him that I would keep him informed.

With each passing day, he never failed to remind me about the impending move of my possessions. It wasn't until after two weeks of relentless reminders that I finally disclosed the pickup and drop-off locations. I had bought some used furniture from Craigslist and paid upfront. Much later, he admitted that my unwavering faith in strangers, evident from paying the full amount without verifying the transaction's authenticity, had truly intrigued him.

The day of the furniture delivery was exhausting, with lots of heavy lifting and sweat. I felt so relieved when I saw Ron coming with an extra person to help. It was then that he told me that the person with him had asked about our financial situation and if we were poor. "Indeed", Ron admitted that we were struggling financially. You see, we were as poor as church mice, metaphorically speaking, but our unwavering faith possessed the strength to conquer even the mightiest mountain on Earth.

It was a remarkable day when I had the honor of witnessing the incredible depth of Ron's humanity and compassion. Despite all the hard work, I decided to show a small act of kindness by offering them a meal, but they humbly declined and chose a refreshing glass of water instead.

In response, Ron expressed, "You are truly exceptional. Your gesture of offering a meal is truly remarkable."

At first, I was a bit puzzled by his reaction until I understood that his cultural background was influencing his behavior. In Africa, sharing food with strangers is a gesture of honor, unlike in the United States where it's not common. Additionally, since I couldn't pay him enough in cash, I opted to give him a $100 check as a token of appreciation for his help.

Two weeks later, I unexpectedly crossed paths with him at the workplace. "You did not really have to pay me," he told me.

Intrigued, I asked, "Why?"

He said, "I feel obliged to give the check back."

Despite my initial hesitance, he insisted on returning the check. In a gesture of appreciation, we shared a warm embrace.

Unexpectedly, a strange sensation washed over me as we hugged - a feeling of melting in his arms. In that moment, everything stood still, and I found myself feeling secure, content, and peaceful. Our connection deepened as we exchanged a kiss, an unforgettable moment filled with an unspoken bond that only our hearts could decipher.

But who was this guy? Curiosity consumed me as I pondered the identity of this mysterious individual. In that moment, my mind was fixated on unraveling the enigma before me.

Little did we realize that this chance meeting would mark the commencement of a captivating love tale. Despite the potential for romance, I found myself grappling with inner turmoil. I still felt broken and unprepared to embrace new connections. The notion of letting my guard down and placing trust in another seemed like an insurmountable challenge.

Our first date was filled with excitement and a bit of nervousness. We met at a park, a neutral public spot. As we sat across from each other, the conversation flowed effortlessly, and laughter filled the air. Our interests, dreams, and values aligned seamlessly, forging an instant connection between us. That's when he shared that he was separated from his wife, who was now his ex.

"We're still living together while I sort things out," he confessed.

This revelation set off alarm bells in my head, but I chose to trust him despite my reservations. It was only recently that I had experienced a comparable, albeit intricate, situation of my own. There was something about him—his openness and vulnerability—that made you want to believe in him. He wore his heart on his sleeve, and it ignited a longing within me to protect it for him. As we wrapped up our first date, he playfully called me 'angel' and flashed a charming smile. He certainly knew how to flirt.

As we continued our romantic rendezvous in parks and restaurants, my heart became more and more smitten. Then, out of the blue, his partner, who had previously believed that no one could ever love him, suddenly saw me as a threat to their relationship. Despite my attempts to distance myself, the arrow of love had already pierced my heart, and we found it impossible to stay apart.

The veil of secrecy remained for the entire period. I remember him accompanying my children and me on a trip to Hershey Park. We were modest and stayed in separate quarters.

It was a typical evening in Jersey when he surprised me with a phone call, just an hour after our usual date had ended. His words caught me off guard as he announced, "I'm coming over to spend the night at your place." Uncertainty filled my mind, unsure whether to feel alarmed or excited by this unexpected turn of events. In the end, he settled for the couch downstairs, and at that moment, I realized he was a true gentleman. I made the conscious choice to allow him to handle his own problems without injecting my two cents.

Ron really stepped up to help us get accustomed to life in America. He introduced us to bologna sandwiches, showed us how to make breakfast potatoes, and even put together our first Thanksgiving dinner. He also bought us our first Christmas tree, a real pine tree, which caused quite a stir back at his home. He was there for the trivial things that meant so much to us. Even though our first meeting did not start on the best foot, it was certainly unforgettable.

Finding love again might seem simple, but keeping a healthy relationship takes work. Trust and open communication are the foundation of any successful relationship. It demands openness, honesty, and vulnerability. We both made a point to be open and honest with each other. We shared our fears and insecurities and created a safe space where we could express our feelings without fear of judgment.

Like every relationship, we have faced our fair share of challenges and setbacks, particularly in the early stages. We approached these obstacles as a team, with abundant patience, understanding, and a willingness to work through them together. Our differences in communication styles and the occasional disagreements surfaced, but we tackled them head-on. We always strove to find common ground and strengthen our bond. However, it is natural after experiencing heartbreak to build walls around one's heart as a shield from potential pain.

Allowing myself to be vulnerable created a space for love. I am glad we both drank from the same cup of this emotion.

One day, when speaking about this intoxicating love, my boyfriend encountered my ex during one of his child visits. He boldly declared, "You know, man, I'm in love with your wife." His audacity was astounding!

As our bond deepened and our connection grew stronger, the topic of starting a family together naturally came up. We delved into our hopes, aspirations, and worries about becoming parents. It was a decision that demanded thoughtful reflection and honest conversations.

I shared, "I felt the need to prove to myself and society, especially in the context of African traditions, that my inability to have a son wasn't my fault as a woman."

My partner added, "I've always longed to have a child of my own to nurture. Circumstances prevented me from raising my own kids, and I do not want my ex-wife to benefit from my social security benefits. I want to have an heir, regardless of gender."

In the end, we both agreed that embracing parenthood would be a wonderful way to further solidify our love.

The gods listened to our pleas and granted our wishes. We were blessed with the gift of pregnancy, but our joy was short-lived as we experienced countless heartbreaking losses. One loss that still haunts us is when we lost our precious child, Aaron, at 21 weeks. We held him in our arms and watched as he took his final breath, his tiny thumb still in his mouth. We held onto hope that he would survive in the NICU, but the doctors shattered our dreams by informing us that the cut-off for viability was at 22 weeks. It still haunts me to this day.

I could not help but think about Anna, our precious child who was lost at 18 weeks. The hospital showed us immense compassion by allowing us to spend a few precious hours with her until her tiny heart ceased to beat. We left with bittersweet memories and cherished photographs, holding onto them tightly. It was during this heartbreaking journey that I received a diagnosis: an incompetent cervix.

As days turned into weeks and weeks into months, I realized that time was not on my side biologically. Desperation filled my heart as I turned to my partner, pleading,

"Can we explore options like IVF, surrogacy, or adoption? Can we find a way to complete our family?" He was having none of it. He had a stubborn streak.

Little did I know that my world would be turned upside down after a routine checkup when I received the devastating diagnosis of cancer. In the upcoming chapter, I will delve deeper into the details. From that point on, my life became a whirlwind of hospital visits, surgeries, radiation sessions, and rounds of chemotherapy. It was a bleak period where hope felt like a distant memory. However, just as I reached rock bottom, a ray of light pierced through the darkness, bringing unexpected news - a tiny life was blossoming within me!

Despite receiving chemotherapy while pregnant, Ethan was born healthy. He's such a firecracker! His infectious energy lights up our days. He entered this world unapologetically. Besides being father and son, they share the same birthday. I could not have wished for more. He's the greatest blessing in my life. I am so thankful for the unexpected turn of events that brought him into our lives.

If I could give any couple struggling to conceive some encouragement, I would say, "I became a mother at the age of 44!"

His dad, my partner, has been my rock and my biggest supporter. He always makes sure I feel like a priority. I often say,

"He treats me like a queen, and most importantly, he always has our backs."

To wrap up this chapter, I want to emphasize that embracing a new beginning or a new love can be a deeply empowering and life-changing experience. It offers a chance to heal from past hurts and to rediscover your value. It is not about erasing the past or replacing what was lost but about moving forward with acceptance. It is an opportunity to write a new chapter in your life.

For you, dearest, find that courage to believe in miracles, hold onto hope, and never give up on your dreams. Of utmost importance, take a leap of faith, trust the path you're on, and welcome the beautiful love that awaits you. For me, that chance encounter blossomed into something beautiful, a bond that transcended time and space.

Chapter 6: The Cancer Diagnosis

AS THE DAY OF MY FIRST chemotherapy session drew near, I could not help but fervently hope that I could somehow evade the entire ordeal. The fact that I was pregnant only added another level of complexity to an already unusual day.

Before my scheduled appointment, I tried to keep my mind off things by sorting out paperwork for my tax returns and looking for any distractions I could find. Time got away from me, though, and suddenly, I had barely any time left for personal hygiene and preparation before my 1 o'clock appointment. Luckily, my partner, adept at navigating through challenges, managed to get us there just in time.

Just in the nick of time, with barely eight minutes to spare, I took a deep breath, said a quiet prayer, and mustered up the bravery to walk into the center. From registering to triage, and then to getting my blood drawn, I could not shake the feeling of being like a fish out of water as I entered the infusion room. Standing by my side was my rock-solid partner, offering unwavering support. The room was alive with energy, with staff members hurriedly eating lunch at a table, gearing up to tackle the rest of the day.

As I entered the infusion room, I could not help but notice the patients hooked up to IV machines. Their curious eyes met mine, but I hesitated to meet their gazes. Being visibly pregnant made me stand out, and I could feel the suspicion in their glances. Thankfully, we stumbled upon a nursing station with a single chair, and I eagerly collapsed into it, feeling utterly drained.

Throughout that period, fatigue and a lack of energy seemed to be my constant companions.

A nurse, returning from a brief break, called out reluctantly, "May I assist you?"

Her demeanor conveyed a sense of annoyance. My partner responded with a touch of attitude, stating our purpose for being there—to undergo chemotherapy. Instructing us to choose an available chemo station, the nurse assured us that someone would attend to us shortly.

After a while, another nurse came over, introduced herself, and confirmed my details. I tried to distract myself by watching a documentary series playing on the TV, but it did little to ease my anxiety. The whole situation felt like a rite of passage, something that no amount of preparation could fully prepare you for. Consulting Dr. Google and WebMD only served to intensify my sense of uncertainty. Reading through the pages only made me certain that I was inflicted with more than one kind of ailment.

Soon, the nurse came back carrying a tray with the medications I needed and started explaining the procedure. One of the drugs was a steroid, and feeling a bit nervous, I gathered the courage to ask if it was safe to use during pregnancy.

"Excuse me?" She responded; her voice raised. I repeated my question, asking whether it was contraindicated for pregnant women.

"Are you pregnant?" She blurted out. The room fell silent, all eyes turning to me. Feeling embarrassed, I averted my gaze and meekly confirmed my pregnancy.

As she walked away, she called out that if I was indeed pregnant, I should not receive the steroid, but she would consult the doctor to confirm. I was overcome with mortification. As the nurse's response echoed in my mind, questions raced through my thoughts.

Shouldn't they have reviewed my medical history and confirmed important details beforehand? Who had ordered the steroid anyway? Uncertainty gnawed at me as the infusions commenced without the administration of steroids.

Unsure of what to anticipate, I began to experience tingling sensations in my feet, accompanied by itchiness in my nasal passage and watery eyes. A heavy cloud seemed to settle upon my head as if I were trapped beneath a lead jacket and helmet. The helmet felt tightly affixed to my scalp, giving me the sensation of pins and needles. A dull headache gradually descended upon me, leaving me bewildered. Had I just signed away from my life?

About forty-five minutes later, we left the center and stopped at a few places on the way home. It was hard for me to pin down exactly how I was feeling. A persistent headache nagged at me while alternating sensations of cold and heat coursed through my body.

Upon reaching home, a sudden craving for boiled eggs struck me, prompting me to request them despite my wavering appetite. Oddly enough, once the eggs were in front of me, my hunger had dissipated into thin air, and I had lost my appetite for this newfound delicacy. Yet, it was as though my body and mind were playing a perplexing game of tug-of-war, leaving me bewildered and unsettled.

As the moon cast a soft glow through the window, I found myself tossing and turning in bed, torn between the discomfort of frequent bathroom visits and the concern about my bladder's health. "Was this a sign of bladder irritation?" I wondered loudly.

As the night dragged on, time seemed to stretch endlessly, with every passing minute feeling like an hour in the quiet solitude of my room. Amidst my restlessness, a soft and delicate sensation stirred within me, akin to a graceful butterfly dancing in my belly. It was the first time I had felt the baby move! However, each flutter carried a subtle plea for comfort, prompting me to offer prayers silently. With each gentle movement, a wave of emotions washed over me, serving as a constant reminder of the precious life blossoming inside.

As the night wore on, plagued by unsettling dreams and the persistent urge to relieve my full bladder, I sought refuge in silent petitions whispered into the stillness of the night.

When the first light of dawn crept into the room, I was already wide awake, the exhaustion pulling at my eyelids contrasting with the relief of having navigated through the long, arduous night. As the world slowly awoke around me, I was relieved that I had made it through the night.

The next day, as the clock struck 4:30 p.m., I settled into the familiar chair in the infusion room, ready for my Neulasta injection. The nurse prepared the syringe, her gentle smile bringing a sense of comfort amidst the clinical surroundings. I closed my eyes, bracing myself for the pain. This injection was meant to boost the inevitable drop in my white blood cell count. This would be a recurring event every three weeks. Whenever I sat in the infusion room surrounded by other patients, each fighting their own battles, I felt a unique bond with these resilient souls. The soft hum of machines and the silent conversations created a backdrop of solidarity, uniting us in our shared journey of healing.

Despite the uncertainty that loomed with each treatment, there was palpable strength in the air. The unwavering determination of my fellow cancer warriors fueled my resolve to conquer the odds stacked against us.

I had no idea that my battle with cancer would begin when I finally mustered up the courage to go for a routine mammogram. Unbeknownst to me, the doctor's order for this crucial test had been tucked away in my car's glove box for the past six months. Being a devoted mother of three, I often prioritized my children's well-being over my own health.

No red flags or cancer history prompted me to schedule a mammogram. I saw it as a routine task to complete. I anticipated a clean bill of health and a return to my daily routine after the appointment. Little did I know fate had something else in store for me.

Stepping into the clinic, the air was heavy with the sterile scent of antiseptic; I could not shake off a growing sense of unease. The waiting room, sparsely populated, was filled with women sitting nervously, their expressions reflecting a mix of apprehension and hope. Finding a seat, I attempted to distract myself with my phone, repeatedly assuring myself that everything would be fine eventually.

Finally, my name was called, and I followed the nurse into the examination room, where a mammography technologist awaited me. The dimly lit room matched the gravity of the situation, and as I undressed and positioned myself in front of the machine, a profound vulnerability and fear enveloped me.

The technologist, exuding a calm and reassuring demeanor, carefully explained the procedure and guided me through each step. While the mammogram itself wasn't uncomfortable, I understood its significance for my well-being. After the procedure, I hurriedly dressed and returned to the waiting room. My heart was filled with anticipation and anxiety as I awaited the results. Time felt like it had stopped, and all I could think about was what the results would be.

Shortly after, the compassionate sonographer put my mind at ease by confirming that everything looked good and there was no cause for concern. She mentioned that the detailed report would be forwarded to my doctor, and her soothing presence helped ease my anxiety. However, my sense of relief was short-lived. Just a few days later, my doctor reached out to me with concerning news. They had discovered a lump and recommended that I return for a more thorough examination.

I was caught off guard, particularly because I recalled the sonographer's initial comforting words during the initial screening. The contradictory information left me feeling overwhelmed. I was anxious and uncertain about the implications for my well-being. Now, in light of this uncertainty, the next course of action was to arrange a follow-up appointment and have a more in-depth conversation with my doctor to gain clarity on the situation.

Upon reaching the scheduled appointment, I encountered the sonographer once more. While she led me through the imaging, my concerns were validated as the presence of a lump became undeniable. This visual confirmation intensified the gravity of the situation, burdening my emotions.

Upon completion of the scan, the sonographer presented me with two choices, each carrying its own set of consequences. I carefully considered my options. The first choice entailed waiting six months for a follow-up scan to monitor any significant changes, while the second option involved undergoing a biopsy, a more invasive procedure that would provide a conclusive diagnosis.

Considering the information at hand and the lack of concerning symptoms or a family history of cancer, I was inclined towards the saying, "Why fix something that isn't broken?" This viewpoint influenced my decision to exercise patience and wait for a period of six months. I carefully evaluated the potential risks and benefits of each option, considering the discomfort that may arise from a biopsy.

With a strong sense of determination, I booked a follow-up appointment with the healthcare experts half a year down the line. It was a moment that made me proud of my choice and optimistic about the journey ahead.

Fortunate to have a compassionate primary care physician, she was not willing to wait six months. Feeling a sense of urgency, she quickly booked a consultation with a specialist in Breast cancer. The specialist meticulously reviewed the results and the various choices at hand, voicing her apprehension with these words, "I cannot confidently suggest waiting for six months. What if the situation worsens unexpectedly?" Her words resonated with me, sparking a renewed sense of urgency and a greater understanding of the importance of proactive healthcare.

Her words struck a chord with me, resonating in the deepest corners of my mind. I could not help but agree with the logic she presented. Though I struggled to grasp every detail, I could not reject the undeniable gravity of the situation unfolding before me. With a heavy yet stubborn heart, I decided to schedule an appointment for the biopsy. The thought lingered like a shadow, casting a mix of fear and hope in my heart. The unknown loomed large, shrouded in uncertainty.

As the day of the biopsy drew closer, my anxiety swelled like a tidal wave about to crash. Stories of the procedure haunted my thoughts, painting vivid images of pain and discomfort. Doubt crept into my mind, overshadowing any semblance of courage I tried to muster. I reminded myself that countless others had walked this path before me, facing their fears head-on. This was merely a routine procedure, a chapter in a story written by thousands every day.

I sat nervously in the waiting room, my palms clammy and my heart racing a marathon. This wasn't how I had imagined my week starting. As my name echoed through the room, I mustered the last ounce of courage I had and rose from my seat, trailing the nurse like a lost puppy. The doctor, with a calming voice that felt like a warm hug, explained the intricate process of the biopsy to me. I tried to focus, I really did, but my mind was elsewhere, lost in a labyrinth of worst-case scenarios. The fear of the unknown gnawed at me like a persistent rodent.

As the doctor started the procedure, I braced myself for the anticipated surge of pain that had been preying on my thoughts. Surprisingly, the sensation wasn't as ghastly as the horror stories my mind had concocted. There was discomfort, yes, but it was bearable, like a splinter lodged under the skin rather than a dagger through the heart.

Lying there, staring at the ceiling tiles that seemed to mock me with their unblemished perfection, I tried to fill the void of silence with positive affirmations. What are the chances of this ordeal culminating in the diagnosis? I mustered in my mind. "As slim as winning the lottery or taking a spontaneous trip to Mars!" my mind reassured. I silently chuckled at the analogy, and just like that, the fear that had gripped me like a vice began to loosen its hold, allowing a sliver of hope to trickle in.

Before I knew it, the procedure was over, and I felt a huge sense of relief. Now, all that was left was to wait for the results, hoping and praying for the best.

During a routine visit to my doctor's office, after I found myself plagued by unusual fatigue and discomfort, I decided to inquire about the status of my biopsy results casually. The atmosphere in the room felt heavy with anticipation as my doctor, engrossed in her computer screen, finally turned to me absent-mindedly and delivered a shocking response, "Yes, it is positive."

With a confused expression, I vehemently expressed my disbelief, yelling out, "No, it can't be true! I can't possibly be pregnant. What are you talking about?"

Realizing the mix-up, my doctor met my gaze and quickly clarified the situation. She explained that the biopsy had detected cancer cells. Acknowledging her limited expertise in this area, she assured me she would contact the breast specialist's office to arrange a follow-up.

"Positive? "Her words hit me like a ton of bricks, causing my heart to race with fear. How could this be real? The news from my doctor was like a heavy blow, leaving me in shock and confusion. Suddenly, my whole world seemed to crumble before my eyes. The gravity of my condition was overwhelming. How serious was it? How long did I have left?

The haunting echoes of these troubling questions echoed in my head, consuming every thought. A deep fear and unease took hold of me as I wondered if there was a mistake in my test results. Exiting the doctor's office, I drifted aimlessly, feeling like a shell of my former self.

Finding comfort in my car, I escaped the tidal wave of emotions crashing over me. Tears streamed down my cheeks as worries about my children's well-being flooded my mind. Adrift in a sea of uncertainties, I drove aimlessly through the town, grappling with the heaviness of my situation and the relentless passage of time. While parked in my car, raindrops began to fall, blending with the storm of emotions swirling inside me. In the distance, thunder rumbled, reflecting the inner chaos that clouded my thoughts.

The thought of my children having to navigate their future without my love and support weighed heavily on me. As a parent, their happiness and security were my primary concerns. The idea of having to reveal this distressing news to my family felt like an immense responsibility. I struggled to find the right words to convey the fear and pain I was experiencing. Knowing that my loved ones would be deeply affected by this diagnosis made the situation even more serious.

I was acutely aware of my condition's profound impact on their lives, forever altering the trajectory of our shared journey and challenging the essence of the American dream we had strived for. Everything that I had dreamed of seemed to be drifting away.

It took me a while to compose myself, but I eventually picked up the phone to call my significant other. Worried about my state of mind, the first thing he asked was, "Where are you? Are you alright?" He was ready to drop everything and come to me right away. I reassured him that I would be okay and told him there was no need to hurry.

Realizing I needed some extra support, I reached out to two other important people. The first person I contacted was my supervisor, to whom I explained my situation. I let them know that I needed some time off but promised to keep them informed. My supervisor showed empathy and reassured me of their support through this challenging time.

My last call was to my pastor's number. Her soothing voice greeted me, and I couldn't stop my tears as I shared my concerns with her. She listened attentively, providing words of comfort and support. Her peaceful presence on the other end of the line brought me the much-needed calm I was looking for at that moment.

"Don't forget to stay resilient and trust in God," she gently reminded me. "He is by your side through it all, and He will never forsake you." Together, we bowed our heads in prayer, seeking strength, courage, and healing. My pastor's words were like a soothing balm to my weary soul, filling me with hope and renewed faith.

Finishing up the three phone calls, I suddenly understood that my understanding of my diagnosis was severely lacking. I realized that my knowledge was only skin-deep. Besides the basics, I was completely clueless. It was like standing on the edge of an endless ocean, unaware of what lurked below.

As I reflected on the bits and pieces of information I had gathered so far, it struck me that beyond just knowing the location of the cancer, there were vital details that were crucial in understanding its seriousness. The specific type of cancer, the stage it was in – these nuances were like puzzle pieces waiting to be put together, creating a more detailed and complete picture. In that moment of complete clarity, I made a conscious decision to stop any further conversations about my condition. It wasn't a way of denying the situation, but rather a hunger for accurate information. I wanted to arm myself with a wealth of knowledge before diving into the realm of treatment options.

I decided to take matters into my own hands and reached out to the breast surgeon's office directly. To my disappointment, the doctor I had seen before was unavailable. Nevertheless, the staff assured me that they would arrange for another doctor to get in touch with me once she completed her surgery. I anxiously awaited the call from this new doctor, desperately hoping that she would provide the valuable information and guidance I needed for my condition.

As promised, the call came through just like they said it would. It brought me reassurance and confirmed that my scheduled visit with the doctor was still on track. It wasn't an easy choice, but with a heavy heart, I decided to take some time off from work and put my health first.

My medical team recommended that I right away undergo lumpectomy surgery, which involved removing the tumor from my breast and extracting lymph nodes for further testing. Thankfully, the surgery was a success and went smoothly. When I received the lab results, the diagnosis of "metastatic triple-positive breast cancer" echoed in my thoughts like a chilling tune. Sitting in the doctor's office, the ticking of the clock seemed to match the beat of my anxious heart. Despite the gravity of the situation, I was resolute in facing this illness with unwavering determination.

My daydream was abruptly interrupted when the door squeaked open, revealing a figure draped in a white coat. The oncologist addressed all my lingering questions and detailed the course of treatment, each word offering a glimmer of hope. The oncologist's voice would soon become a reassuring presence in the midst of my stormy sea of doubt. Was this where I would confront my unwavering adversary?

After allowing myself ample time to heal from the lumpectomy, I embarked on the next phase of my treatment: radiation therapy. As I stepped into the sterile room for my first radiation session, I could not help but feel a rush of mixed emotions. The humming machines and stern-faced technicians painted a stark contrast to the warmth and comfort I craved at that moment. Even in that clinical environment, a glimmer of hope sparked inside me - the hope for a cancer-free future.

As the treatment commenced, an intriguing sense of duality enveloped me with each subsequent session. On one side, the relentless beams of radiation valiantly fought against the treacherous cancer cells, engaging in a vital battle within my own being. However, simultaneously, these very beams sapped away my energy, leaving me feeling utterly drained and fatigued.

After completing the last session, I left the treatment room feeling physically drained but emotionally empowered. Despite the tough side effects, such as burns and blisters, my inner strength shone through with a newfound sense of hope. I was determined to keep fighting and emerge victorious.

Besides my appointment, there was another one set up for the port insertion at the same location. This port would simplify the process of giving chemotherapy drugs and drawing blood. Prior to the placement of the port, a pregnancy test was required. Luckily, the results came back negative, allowing me to move forward with the port insertion smoothly.

I recall the theater nurse asking, "You did a pregnancy test, and the result was..."

"Pregnant with twins," I quipped. His face showed surprise before he caught on to the joke.

Throughout my healing journey, the heavy load of past regrets and lost opportunities gradually lifted. Rather than fixating on insurance policies and long-term goals, I learned to savor the beauty of living in the now. My identity was no longer tied to material wealth and stability. I found delight in the little mishaps of daily life and comfort in the pure happiness that simple pleasures bring. Surrounded by those I hold dear; I treasured every moment we spent together as a precious treasure.

Embracing a healthier lifestyle, I stumbled upon the sheer delight of preparing wholesome vegetable dishes and relishing numerous refreshing glasses of homemade juices. At long last, I had attained the perfect equilibrium between my physical well-being and inner peace that had eluded me for so long.

I immersed myself in reading, deepening my spiritual connection, and found unparalleled tranquility. I also found solace in accepting that my partner and I might not be able to have a child together. The chemotherapy medicines were likely to cause me to go into menopause prematurely. This shift in perspective allowed us to focus on the present moment and the affection we had.

As I embarked on my chemotherapy treatment, I prepared myself for the challenges that awaited - a fight not just against cancer, but against my very core, both physically and mentally. The medications would take a toll on my body, wreaking havoc on both cancerous and my healthy cells.

The inevitability of losing my hair loomed over me like a dark cloud, threatening to strip away not just my locks but also a part of my identity. Faced with this imminent transformation, I refused to succumb to despair. Instead, I embarked on a quest to reclaim ownership of my appearance. I scoured shops and websites, seeking out an array of headscarves, wigs, and stylish hats that would serve as my armor in this battle against self-doubt. Each piece I selected was more than a mere accessory; it was a talisman of my resilience, a declaration of my unwavering spirit.

The side effects of chemotherapy hit me like a relentless storm - waves of nausea, tides of fatigue, and a relentless pounding on my immune system. Simple tasks became monumental challenges. Even everyday activities felt like huge tasks. I do not know how I found the strength to keep going; the unwavering support of my family was all I needed in the darkest of times. The compassionate care of my medical team became a lifeline, guiding me through the tumultuous waters of treatment with expert hands and kind hearts.

I also discovered how helpful and inspiring support groups and fellow cancer warriors can be! Talking with others walking similar paths and sharing our stories, fears, and victories provided a sense of community and motivation. I realized that I was not alone in this fight. The camaraderie we shared was a powerful force, knitting us together in a tapestry of shared experiences, fears, and triumphs. Each tale of struggle and survival added to the collective strength of our group, bolstering our resolve to keep pushing forward, no matter how steep the mountain before us. In the embrace of these kindred souls, I found solace and inspiration. Their unwavering support lifted me on the days when my courage wavered, and their words of encouragement functioned as a salve for my weary soul. Together, we stood as warriors, united in our battle against a common enemy, finding strength in our shared vulnerabilities and victories.

As I look back on my journey through the shadows of cancer, I am awestruck by the resilience of the human spirit. The trials I faced tested me in ways I had never imagined, but in the crucible of adversity, I discovered a wellspring of strength within myself. Each day became a canvas on which I painted my determination to live fiercely, love deeply, and find joy in the simplest of moments.

Cancer may have altered the course of my life, but it did not define my essence. Emerging from the crucible of suffering, I carry with me a renewed purpose – to spread the message of hope, to raise awareness about the importance of early detection, and to remind others of the precious gift of self-care.

In the tapestry of my life, the threads of pain and struggle are interwoven with those of resilience, compassion, and hope. As I continue to walk this path, I do so with a heart full of gratitude for the support groups and fellow warriors who illuminated my way with their unwavering light.

Chapter 7: The Pregnancy

EXPERIENCING PREGNANCY while battling cancer is an incredibly daunting and demanding circumstance. It's a sensitive situation that demands careful handling. I've come to understand that open conversations with healthcare providers are essential, as well as the unwavering encouragement from family and friends. Every decision made during this time has a far-reaching impact, influencing not only the mother's health but also that of her beloved baby.

As my partner and I discussed our inability to conceive a child, a sense of tranquility washed over me. In the past, I had exhausted every effort to persuade him to consider alternatives like surrogacy or using a donor's egg or embryo, but he remained resolute. Just when I believed things couldn't deteriorate further, the devastating blow of a cancer diagnosis shattered my hopes of experiencing motherhood once more. Following surgery and radiation, my sole concentration shifted towards battling cancer, and the thought of pregnancy became a distant memory.

Life has a way of surprising us with its twists and turns. As I ventured into Walmart on the eve of Halloween, my main mission was to find the perfect Halloween costumes and candies for my daughter. Little did I know that fate had a different plan in store for me. In a spontaneous moment, I found myself drawn towards the pharmacy aisle, where an array of pregnancy test kits awaited my attention. Even though I had received a negative result from a test just a week ago, an inexplicable urge compelled me to take one home with me.

After running a few errands, I finally found myself at home with the much-needed privacy to take the pregnancy test. As I anxiously awaited the result, my mind couldn't help but wander to those lucky lottery winners who impulsively purchase a ticket, never anticipating the immense changes that await them. Little did I realize that this seemingly innocent impulse of mine would forever reshape the trajectory of my life.

After testing and reading numerous pregnancy tests, I became adept at spotting a positive result early on, before it became very obvious. Fortunately, this time, the positive line appeared stronger than the control line within a few seconds.

The realization was so intense, it felt like a ton of bricks crashing down on me, leaving me completely stunned! Looking back, this was the one time I didn't have to squint my eyes against a light, hoping that a barely detectable or seemingly missing positive line would miraculously appear.

A whirlwind of emotions engulfed me, leaving me unsure of how to react. Should I embrace happiness, shock, excitement, exhilaration, joy, or simply let the tears flow? Surprisingly, none of these options seemed fitting as I found myself bursting into uncontrollable laughter, echoing through the confines of the restroom. The laughter seemed endless, refusing to subside. In that moment, all I could ponder was, "Oh, how you must have a wicked sense of humor, dear God! Why, oh Lord, did this become an epi-climax? Just a week ago, a chemo port had been implanted, and I had mentally prepared myself for the upcoming chemotherapy sessions."

Bursting with laughter, I dashed outside to find my partner. He was on the phone, but abruptly ended the call, clearly concerned by my fits of giggles. He must have assumed something serious was happening. In the midst of my laughter, I handed him the pregnancy test.

He glanced at the test, then turned his gaze towards me. "What's this?" he inquired.

"It's a positive pregnancy test," I responded, still chuckling uncontrollably.

I could see the realization dawning in his eyes. Having experienced the trials of testing for years, he was all too familiar with its meaning.

"Of course, I know what it is, but who does it belong to?" he asked.

"I just tested it a few minutes ago," I replied.

After getting over the initial shock, all I could see on his face was concern and many unvoiced questions.

As memories flooded my thoughts, I could sense what he was thinking. The excitement of finding out we were pregnant in 2015, the hopes and dreams we had shared shattered by a first-trimester loss. The anguish of 2016 when we lost our baby boy at 21 weeks, a perfect little life taken too soon by an incompetent cervix. The devastation of 2017 when we said goodbye to another precious soul at 18 weeks, a genetic disorder stealing our chance at happiness once more.

As the weight of reality sank in, I found myself frozen in place, a whirlwind of emotions and questions raging inside me. The unexpected news of my pregnancy had intertwined my happiness with the looming presence of my ongoing battle against cancer.

Can I proceed with my treatment while pregnant, or is it better to pause? What would the doctor advise? Will chemotherapy affect the little life growing inside me? What are the potential dangers for both me and the baby? Why is all of this happening? These uncertainties lingered in my thoughts, creating obstacles to finding answers.

As I grappled with this unexpected intersection of life and uncertainty, I found myself torn between the desperate need to fight my illness and the fierce instinct to protect the child growing inside me. The road ahead seemed shrouded in fog, with no clear path to guide me. Feeling lost, I found myself at a crossroads. Uncertainty clouded my mind as confusion became my constant companion.

As weeks passed by, I found myself stuck in a state of uncertainty, deciding to take a "wait and see" stance. The gravity of the situation caused me to shy away from facing the truth with my oncology team. Nevertheless, when I reached around seven weeks into my pregnancy, a newfound sense of resolve pushed me to reach out for assistance.

With shaky hands, I dialed the number of a high-risk pregnancy unit, hoping for guidance. To my dismay, they required a doctor's diagnosis, or a pregnancy note to proceed. Desperation kicked in as I reached out to community service organizations specializing in women's health care. The visit unfolded like a whirlwind - paperwork, counseling, scripture reading, prayers, and then the moment of truth: the ultrasound.

As the monitor flickered to life, my heart skipped a beat. Tears welled up in my eyes as the image of a tiny being with a strong heartbeat filled the screen. Joy and gratitude flooded my soul as I realized that within me, a precious life was thriving against all odds.

The prayers and support offered by the center became a ray of light in my darkest hour. Today, as I pen down these words, I reflect on the twists and turns that brought me to this moment of profound gratitude. I remain forever indebted to this community service center for their unwavering support and the precious gift of reassurance they bestowed upon me in my time of need.

With my ultrasound documents in hand, I called the high-risk clinic again. I waited anxiously for them to call back and schedule an appointment. Eventually, I received a call back from the case manager. She informed me that, after consulting with the gynecological team, they had recommended that I terminate the pregnancy due to my cancer diagnosis. Furthermore, she noted that since my medical insurance was on file, I did not need to worry about payment.

I was shocked beyond words and even more stunned that this pro-life health establishment would endorse this path. I felt alone and unsure of what to do next, and I broke down in tears. As I gazed out of the window, the world seemed to blur into a haze of uncertainty. The whispers of doubt and fear echoed in my mind, drowning out everything else. How could I choose between my life and the life growing within me?

Finding the right words to convey the turmoil of emotions I was experiencing felt nearly impossible. Amid sobs, I raised my eyes to my Lord and Savior, asking why this test was happening now. Then, I recalled the following passage from the New International Version (NIV) of Psalm 121: "I lift my eyes to the mountains—where does my help come from? My help comes from the LORD, the Maker of heaven and earth."

Throughout my journey with the diagnosis and the ensuing challenges, my relationship with God had been renewed. Instead of asking, "Why me, Lord?" or asking God to take away my suffering, I had invited Him to walk by my side, inviting Him into my storm. I understood that there is no testimony without a test. Just as He had walked alongside Moses, Jacob, Joseph, Daniel, and many other significant biblical characters, I believed he would see me through this.

As all of this was going on, I had three doctor's visits scheduled: one with my breast surgeon, who happened to be linked with the health system that was closing doors on me, and two with oncologists. One of the oncologists was unquestionably on my treatment team, while the other had been consulted for a second opinion.

The consultation appointment came first. My doctor congratulated me on my pregnancy but was emphatic that the best course of action was to terminate it and begin treatment right away. She talked about how she had lost patients who had chosen to maintain the pregnancy, and their conditions had quickly deteriorated. She presented me with two painful choices: to have the baby and possibly not survive to care for it and my other three beautiful children or to live for the sake of my living children. If I chose to go with her, she already had a treatment plan in place.

As I exited the doctor's office that afternoon, I could not shake the haunting memory of her chilling words. The atmosphere in the room had been oppressive, the weight of the decision hanging heavily in the air. It was a decision that no mother should ever be forced to confront - to choose between the life blossoming inside her and the opportunity to care for the children she already cherished so deeply. The mere thought of releasing the precious life within me was inconceivable, a little soul that had already captured my heart in a way I never thought possible.

The doctor's words continued to echo in my mind as I stood outside her office. Her demeanor was professional, her words serious, and her gaze heavy with the burden of experience - filled with the weight of the lives she had seen slip away. The choice ahead of me was daunting, weighing the life within me against the lives already in my care. The decision loomed large, leaving me lost in contemplation.

So, there and then, with trembling hands and a resolve born of a mother's love, I canceled all future appointments with the doctor who had who presented my options so coldly. As I walked away from the sterile corridors of the hospital, my heart was heavy, but my spirit remained unbowed. In that moment, I had chosen the less-traveled path, a road fraught with uncertainty but lined with the unparalleled joy of a mother's sacrifice.

My next appointment was with the breast surgeon, and everything went far better than I had hoped. After all the formalities were completed, she shared a piece of news that changed everything.

"Chemotherapy can be given to pregnant women," she informed me. "I don't know why my colleagues are recommending termination!"

This news was a relief. I no longer had to worry about terminating my pregnancy. As if in a perfect Christmas tale, this news came just around the corner of the holiday, making it the best present I could have asked for. My oncologist was the last of the three appointments, which had to be rescheduled due to the Christmas holiday.

In the midst of a stormy ocean of fear and doubt, haunting memories of previous miscarriages and a gloomy future resurfaced within me. Every slight ache or sniffle triggered a whirlwind of worry in my mind, anticipating the worst. With no gynecologist appointment on the horizon, I felt lost in a vast expanse of anxiety.

In the following weeks, I found myself returning to the community center multiple times for additional ultrasounds, clinging to any glimmer of hope they offered. The staff began to notice and expressed their concerns about my well-being. Then, on a significant day, I sought support from a caring counselor. I opened up about my fears and challenges, including the daunting suggestion of terminating the pregnancy, the haunting memories of previous losses, and the feeling of being turned away when I needed help the most. It was disheartening to discover that the high-risk unit had refused to admit me and turned me away.

Moved by compassion, the counselor proceeded with the ultrasound. As the screen flickered to life, revealing my little one squirming and thriving within me, a glimmer of hope pierced through the darkness that had clouded my mind. I made a silent vow to protect and cherish this fragile existence growing within me, come what may.

The counselor discussed this with her colleagues. One woman pointed out that they had a doctor on their team and promised to bring up my situation with her. At that point, I wasn't worried about what type of doctor she was or her area of expertise, whether she specialized in dermatology or not. All I wanted was a caring expert to hear me out.

As I made my regular visits to the center, I could not help but notice the unwavering warmth and compassion radiating from the women there. Their faces were aglow with empathy, making me feel truly understood. With the Christmas season approaching, their kindness filled my heart with an unexpected sense of hope and cheer.

"Who am I to decide to terminate this precious life for which I had prayed and fasted for so long?" I asked myself. Talk about divine timing; it felt as if God was leading me through this.

Several days later, the community center contacted me by phone, requesting more details about my condition to pass on to the doctor. Despite never having met her face-to-face, this mysterious doctor ended up playing a crucial role in my medical journey—a true game-changer.

I discovered that Progesterone and Estrogen were contributing to my cancer from a medical standpoint. In other words, my breast cancer had a high number of estrogen and progesterone receptors, leading to its classification as hormone-receptor-positive, also known as PR/ER +. The chemotherapy I needed aimed to prevent the cancer from coming back by blocking the effects of these two hormones. However, getting pregnant could increase the levels of these hormones, potentially fueling the growth of the disease or raising the chances of it returning after treatment.

I was all set for my third appointment with my primary oncologist. I could not help but feel a bit anxious about what this visit had in store for me. Since I had to cancel my first infusion, I had already fallen behind on my therapy. As we began our conversation, she could not contain her excitement while recounting an incident where she received a phone call from a renowned oncologist while returning from a family vacation. It was so unexpected that she had to quickly pull over to the side of the road just to speak with the caller. I had a hunch that this caller might be someone important, perhaps even the head of the Oncology Board Review in New Jersey.

My oncologist said that their conversation had centered on this pregnant cancer patient—me. She determined that the second oncologist's recommendation for termination was completely unjustified. I'll never know how she learned about the talk I had with the consultant oncologist. However, an anonymous pro bono oncology executive provided my oncologist with peer-reviewed studies that revealed no disparities between women who underwent chemotherapy treatment during pregnancy and those who chose to terminate their pregnancies.

It was quite surprising to hear her admit that she had never dealt with a pregnant woman needing chemotherapy before. However, she assured me that she would consult with other experts and delve deeper into modifying the treatment or protocol. To proceed, I needed to seek the approval of a gynecologist who would give me the green light to begin chemotherapy during my second trimester.

The mysterious doctor referred to me by a compassionate counselor from the Community Service Center will always be an enigma. However, one thing I can say for certain is that this doctor turned out to be a top-notch oncologist, not a dermatologist or anything else.

In the midst of challenging times, I witnessed the splendor, magnificence, and grandeur of God more vividly than before. God pledges to stand by our side, providing protection and guidance. His plans for us are enduring, not fleeting. He guarantees that He will walk alongside us for the long haul. I had unquestionably transformed into my own self-motivation guru.

I felt a profound sense of relief, as if I had been given a new lease on life. With renewed determination, I called the high-risk unit once more. I was desperate for the opportunity to fight for my baby and to allow God to work through me. After some back-and-forth communication, and with the assistance of a counselor I had requested, I was able to secure my first appointment, which was labeled as a consultation.

On the day of my consultation, I encountered a doctor from a prior pregnancy. To begin, my connection with this doctor had not been easy, according to my mental medical records. In one of my previous miscarriages, chromosomal abnormalities were discovered during a routine blood test and a 14-week ultrasound. The results suggested that something was wrong. The doctor had recommended a more invasive test called an amniocentesis. I knew this test was part of the standard practice, but I still rejected it.

In 2017, I found this test unnecessary as it seemed to serve no purpose other than validating a research kit being developed by a doctor who was a research resident at the time. Due to the potential risks, I respectfully refused. I opted to wait for the detailed anatomy scan scheduled for weeks 18-20. The pivotal moment came during the 18-week scan when an anomaly was clearly detected.

As if on cue, the doctor reappeared, this time accompanied by a professor, and explained the diagnosis. Seeing me as the ideal subject, the doctor advised that I consider obtaining an amniocentesis test. Really? For what reason? I was furious. Why would I put myself through such a terrible operation when we already knew the diagnosis and prognosis? So that you can work on developing your research kit? This was not going to alter my baby's fate. So, once again, my response was, "Thank you, but no." My emotions were strong at the moment, and the pain in my heart was unbearable.

"I want to make it clear, doctor, that despite my current state on this examination bed, identified as of certain ancestry, I work in the medical field," I continued with emotion in my voice.

"Considering all that, my final answer is no." I was relieved to see that he remembered our previous encounter.

As we delved into my medical history and discussed the potential path forward, the phrase "all odds appear to be stacked against you" echoed in my thoughts like a haunting melody. At 43 years old, the journey to conceive and carry a baby to term was already an enormous challenge. Reflecting on my past pregnancy complications, along with a genetic disorder and numerous unfavorable outcomes, I couldn't help but feel overwhelmed.

As my mind whirled, doubts crept in, and I could not help but question myself. Was I naive to even entertain this idea? Was I being unrealistic in my aspirations? Were my hopes of expanding my family mere illusions in the face of such daunting odds? The uncertainty ate away at me, sending my thoughts into a chaotic whirlwind.

The fear of invasive testing had always been at the back of my mind, and now it loomed larger than ever. The risks were tangible—the threat of a miscarriage, the pain, the potential infections, the cramps. Could I knowingly put myself in such harm's way?

Then again, I had to think about the bigger picture. What if this was my last opportunity to have a child? What if my fears sabotaged my dreams? As I wrestled with these questions, I realized I needed to be brave. I needed to take the necessary steps to ensure a safe and healthy pregnancy.

As I sat opposite my doctor, I took a deep breath and talked about the topic of the next steps. He recommended the same regimen of blood testing and scanning, along with invasive diagnostics at the earliest and prophylactic cerclage. It was a lot to process, but I knew I needed to display resilience. For the sake of my unborn child, I had to confront my fears. This was not just any baby; it felt like a life ordained by God. With that in mind, I consented to all the medical plans.

As the day of my amniocentesis approached, I found myself lying on the hospital bed, and my nerves stretched taut like a bowstring. The mere thought of a fine needle piercing through my belly was enough to send chills down my spine, but the physical discomfort paled in comparison to the fear of potential consequences. Given my history of pregnancy loss due to chromosomal defects, the stakes felt incredibly high. The prospect of losing yet another pregnancy was too horrifying to contemplate.

At the end of the amniocentesis, a wave of anxiety washed over me. The hospital's aftercare instructions repeated in my mind as I left the building, making me feel like I was walking on eggshells. The risk of infections and cramping seemed like a minor inconvenience compared to the terror of possibly losing my baby. The notion of carrying a child with another chromosomal defect felt suffocating. It felt as though I was caught in a ceaseless cycle of fear and despair. The mere idea of not being able to get the cerclage made me feel so hopeless. The burden of this no win situation was unbearable. Finally, the test results arrived after what felt like an eternity of waiting. I could hardly believe my eyes as I read them—my baby had been given a clean bill of health!

Tears of joy welled up and streamed down my face as I realized that I could now proceed with my obstetric visits and get the much-needed cerclage. This overwhelmingly relieving news filled me with a happiness I hadn't felt in a while.

As I scheduled my appointments, I kept reminding myself that I had to do everything in my power to keep this rainbow baby safe and sound. Despite the cancer diagnosis and forthcoming treatments, my primary focus was on ensuring a successful pregnancy. The doctor's prescription for bed rest was one of my routine care measures, and I adhered to it religiously. With each passing day, my affection for my growing baby grew, and I was determined to stop at nothing to ensure the success of this pregnancy.

Looking back on the time when I was approximately 15 weeks pregnant, my heart still races with a mix of anxiety and anticipation. It was during this period that I received the green light to begin chemotherapy, a decision that could have easily gone the other way.

Suddenly, my routine obstetric visits transformed into crucial checkpoints on my survival journey. The schedule was demanding, alternating between chemotherapy sessions and obstetric appointments every two weeks, each presenting its own unique challenges. Regular blood work became a vital necessity, with tests scheduled for days 7 and 14 and just before my next chemo treatment on day 21. As if the pressure wasn't overwhelming, I had to go the extra mile and find a private sonographer to ensure that my baby was growing as expected. It truly became a matter of life or death.

As I entered the 26th week of my pregnancy, an unexpected condition hit me like a bolt of lightning, turning my body into a balloon on the verge of bursting. Looking at myself in the mirror became a challenge, as I could hardly recognize the person staring back at me. The weight, both physical and emotional, felt overwhelming, dragging me down.

Seeking answers, I made my way to the doctor's office, hoping for some clarity. However, instead of finding solace, the shadows lurking in my mind only grew deeper. The news I received shattered my world into a million pieces - the cardiac problems from my chemotherapy sessions had progressed, posing a threat to my pregnancy. Panic surged through me like a tidal wave, threatening to overpower my determination. The words on my script echoed in my head: "Cardiac specialist referral."

With a heavy heart, I sought the expertise of a heart specialist who prescribed a new regimen of medications. However, the whispered threat of pregnancy termination loomed over me like a dark cloud, casting a shadow on the tendrils of hope I had desperately clung to.

Living through this ordeal was nothing less than a nightmare. Even within the walls of my home, there was no relief. Constant nausea, fatigue, and loss of appetite had me confined to my bed for most of the day. Every effort I made, even those as ordinary as tidying up the house or loading and emptying the dishwasher, would leave me gasping for breath. Some days, the level of exhaustion was such that it felt like being run over by a train, leaving me incapable of even moving a bit. I was forced to muster every bit of remaining strength to crawl back to bed. This was a true test of my endurance and fortitude, as I found myself struggling to make it through each day. As if things weren't difficult enough, the arrival of Covid brought another degree of intricacy to my already precarious situation. The act of emotionally dealing with the shutdown, along with the continual onslaught of news reports, instilled a deep terror in me.

The very thought of being pregnant while undergoing chemotherapy during a pandemic was nothing short of overwhelming. The dread of stepping out of the house and potentially exposing myself to this lethal virus was paralyzing. In fact, this meant that my partner was unable to accompany me inside the hospital walls on my doctor's visits. It was clear that I had to take every possible precaution to protect my unborn child and myself. I recall how I would sterilize everything and everyone who entered my house, including myself. The worry of catching Covid grew so strong that I began wearing a face mask to bed every night. It was a risk, but I felt I had no alternative.

On the precipice of the last month of my pregnancy, there was a pause in my chemotherapy. This brought a great sense of relief, considering the horrifying idea of being subjected to chemotherapy while nurturing a life within me.

As summer rolled in and the Fourth of July drew near, a mix of relief and happiness filled the air. But amidst it all, a sense of worry consumed my heart. My daughter's graduation as valedictorian was merely a fortnight away, and the thought of not being able to attend weighed heavily on my mind. The fear of missing out on such a significant milestone gripped me tightly.

Despite our concerns, my family and I are explorers at heart, and we could not bear the notion of sitting at home and wallowing in our fears. We decided to take a gamble and go camping. Our goal was the famed Jersey Shore town of Cape May, which is around 140 miles from our house. Our journey to that place was made in our RV, and the opportunity to inhale the crisp air and savor the picturesque views brought us a much-needed respite. The temporary pause in my chemotherapy treatment provided a wonderful opportunity to embrace this escape from my usual medical routine. However, there was still one obstacle left to overcome: my scheduled obstetric visit on July 5th, which meant I had to make the round trip to Cape May once more.

What ensued was a 300-mile round drive in one day to and from the doctor, a bad decision, and a watershed moment in my life. Sitting inside the RV, my heart pounded in my chest, a surge of uneasiness washing over me. In an instant, it hit me like a bolt of lightning - I was about to go into labor! Panic gripped me tightly, but I fought to keep my composure. As the weight of the situation settled in, I swiftly dialed 911, my pulse racing as I anxiously anticipated the arrival of the ambulance.

Our highly anticipated Memorial vacation joy was abruptly halted on that fateful day. I was swiftly rushed to the nearest hospital as I unexpectedly went into labor. The pain was excruciating, intensifying with every passing moment. Despite my anguish, I understood that I had to hold on, for the well-being of my unborn child. The hours of labor were practically forever, and they remain fresh in my recollection to this day. There was suffering, worry, and a lot of uncertainty, especially as the physicians tried to find and untie the cerclage. I was in the throes of labor for hours, and the sensation was like my body being ripped apart bit by bit. But at 1 a.m., everything took a turn. My tiny newborn son entered the world, weighing just 6.5 pounds yet bursting with vitality. His initial cry was a beautiful symphony of happiness and comfort to my ears. I could sense my partner's emotions as he followed instructions to sever the umbilical cord. Holding him close, I knew instantly that all the challenges and pain had led to this precious moment. He was my brave little fighter.

Despite being born prematurely by four weeks, my baby showed remarkable strength and health. He didn't need to stay in the NICU and appeared ready to embrace the world. It was as if he understood his assignment - the importance of being strong, not only for himself but also for his mother.

It was truly remarkable that he came into this world on his father's special day – his birthday. The sheer significance of his birth aligning with such a momentous occasion was not lost on any of us. It felt like more than just a mere coincidence; it seemed to deepen the unbreakable bond within our family.

It was written in the stars that he would become a part of our family, and we could feel it in our bones! The moment he came into this world felt like a grand cosmic plan, as if the entire universe had conspired to bring us together at this precise moment, filling us with the incredible energy of new beginnings. As we cradled him in our arms, we became acutely aware of the challenges that lay ahead. However, we also recognized that this journey would fortify our bond and unite us even more. As his fourth birthday approaches, we are reminded of the countless blessings he has brought into our lives.

Chapter 8: Against All Odds: Cancer and a baby at 43?

THIS IS GOING TO BE the shortest chapter in my memoir. As you have already read the previous chapters, you already know the outcome.

Becoming pregnant at 43 can be quite challenging for many women. However, life has a tendency to surprise us with unexpected obstacles. As women get older, their fertility decreases, making a pregnancy at 43 quite rare. By the time a woman reaches her early 40s, the likelihood of conceiving naturally diminishes, creating more obstacles along the way. It was my initial strike. Just when I thought things could not get any worse, a cancer diagnosis, treatment, and the looming possibility of early menopause all came crashing down on me.

Cancer and a baby? How could these two coexist? As I grappled with the reality of my situation, a whirlwind of emotions engulfed me. Fear, uncertainty, hope – they all mingled together in a chaotic dance within me. How could I bring a child into this world while fighting a battle for my own life? Would I even be around to see this child grow up? The world seemed to be testing my mettle in a cruel game, putting my resilience and fortitude to the test.

Besides dealing with the decision to keep or abort the pregnancy, the toughest part was yet to come – breaking the news. How would everyone react to this unexpected twist in my life? Amidst the darkness of cancer diagnosis? How would I explain this to my loved ones, coworkers, and, most significantly, my teenage daughters? What would I say if I wanted to - confess that the forbidden fruit of pleasure was still with me? How do I gather my thoughts before breaking the news? I was taken aback! Holy cow! Do I compose myself and announce, "Surprise! Surprise! I am, or we are pregnant! At 43, while trying to be a cancer warrior?" This wasn't going to work.

When I was a kid, my family and I lived in a little African town that wasn't even on Google Maps, so we never had electricity. Our house was contemporary, and it had beds. Yes, mattresses, blankets, and bed sheets. There were two beds in my parents' room. The larger bed was my dad's. My mom shared her bed with nursing babies and the next baby in line. Because I was the firstborn, I used to make up nightmares so I could sleep in my parents' room. From a young age, I never imagined the room would be used for anything other than sleeping. Even after turning 18 and over, my siblings and I would enter that room at any time of the night to talk to our parents. Now, here I was, struggling with the difficulty of breaking this news to my children!

As the clock struck midnight and we bid farewell to 2019, my family and I found ourselves in the lap of luxury at a magnificent ski resort in Jersey. The excitement was palpable as we eagerly anticipated hitting the slopes the next morning. While my kids were bursting with enthusiasm, trying to convince me to join their ski party, my partner and I shared a knowing look. Although I could not partake in the skiing adventure, I found immense joy in simply watching and cheering them on.

I could not contain my laughter as I witnessed my partner take a tumble while attempting to show off his skiing skills on the slope. The onlookers must have thought I was out of my mind. I had been observing him carefully as he made his way down the hill, struggling to maintain control and zigzagging down the trail. I had a feeling of what was about to happen even before it did. I had my camera ready in video mode, waiting for the perfect moment. And then, it happened! Boom! He fell and twisted in a dramatic fashion. All eyes were on him, filled with concern and questions like, "Is he okay?" "Do we need to call for help?" And there I was, a Black woman, trying to stifle my uncontrollable laughter!

One of the staff members said to me, "Are you okay?" which I took to mean both "Are you crazy?" and "How dare you laugh when we have a situation?"

Amidst fits of laughter, I responded, "Absolutely! I'm perfectly alright. He's my husband, and trust me, he'll be absolutely fine!"

My youngest daughter, who was six years old then, remembers this incident and says, "Mummy, I knew it! You were carrying Ethan. That is why you did not want to ski!"

You see, the journey to motherhood can take unexpected turns. The unique challenges and decisions faced by women who find themselves pregnant at a later age are magnified, especially when one is supposed to be fighting for their life rather than being blissful. But such life distractions were so welcome from the shadow of "Am I going to die or survive."

There was a lot of discussion happening behind the scenes. My partner wanted me to tell the children right away, but I was very hesitant. This is not surprising, given that I am a "wait and see" person. However, I was quite concerned from the beginning. What was society's moral standard? Would I be judged harshly?

I had experienced so much pregnancy loss. Now at 43? There was a higher chance of genetic disorders. All status quo – cancer aside and all that - What if pregnancy did not hold?

How should I break the news of my pregnancy to my teenage daughters? How will they react? And what decisions will I have to make? Fear gripped my heart as these questions raced through my mind.

One evening, after mustering up the courage, I gathered my daughters in the living room. Their young faces were filled with anticipation, oblivious to the burden I carried. Tension filled the air, and as I cleared my throat, a sense of unease took over the room.

As I rehearsed the words in my mind, trying to find the right way to share the news, I realized that there was no perfect time, no ideal scenario. So, I took a deep breath again, plastered a smile on my face and said, "Girls, I have something important to share with you," I began, trying to steady my voice. "You see, despite my cancer treatment, I've learned that I'm pregnant."

There was silence in the room, and I glanced at my daughters, searching for signs of understanding. It was as if their young minds were struggling to process the information, their eyes widening in shock.

My eldest daughter, Elsa, found her voice first. "Mom, but you're sick. Can you even have a baby?"

"It is complicated, sweetheart," I replied, my voice a mix of frustration and sadness. "There are risks involved for both me and the baby."

Tears welled up in my younger daughter's eyes. "I knew it! But are you going to keep it?" she asked, her voice quivering.

My heart ached at the pain in her voice. I took a deep breath, my mind racing between choices that held their consequences. "I have two options," I said cautiously. "I can choose to have chemotherapy and terminate the pregnancy, or I can keep the baby and continue with the treatment."

Elsa tried being the more sensible one. "Mom, it is your decision," she said softly. "But we love you, and we'll support you no matter what."

My middle daughter, Elna, did not say anything to me. Later, she cornered my partner and asked, "How could two grown-ups get into such a mess?" She finished by accusing him, "You guys should know better."

As a mother, I knew their young minds could not fully comprehend the situation's complexities. However, their unwavering love and support provided a ray of hope in my darkened world. At that moment, I gained strength to face the uncertain path ahead.

Then, there was the reality of facing medical personnel. "Termination" became a familiar term from the beginning to the middle and the end. I am convinced they believed I was clinging to fast sand. It was inevitable that the pregnancy would end in a miscarriage anyway.

There were worries about the elevated chance of genetic abnormalities in my baby due to my advanced age and medical history. At 12 weeks, we began screening for chromosomal abnormalities with a blood sample. The results were encouraging, which was a relief. I had to get a preventive cerclage. Therefore, we had to get an amniocentesis when I was 14 weeks along. A lot of thought went into this choice. I was told that the physicians would not give me the cerclage if they found anything out of the ordinary. The findings were normal in the end, which eased some of the concerns.

As a woman navigating this new phase, I found solace and strength in my renewed faith. Psalm 121 from the New International Version (NIV) offered words of encouragement and guidance during this challenging time.

I scoured the internet in hopes of finding some comfort. At times, I even splurged on questionably authentic fortune tellers online. But then I stumbled upon one that just sang! Sweetly! Indeed. Yes, I shelled out more than $200 for a thirty-minute session of compassion and empathy.

I had the pleasure of meeting an exceptional woman who ran her own sonography practice. She provided excellent support, conducting ultrasounds weekly, and more often when necessary. During each appointment, she was always comforting and reassuring. All we had to do was give her a heads-up before heading over.

"Can you schedule us in?"

"In an hour? Absolutely," she would say.

I found myself straddling the realms of advanced maternal age and battling cancer at a young age. The obstetric visits, scheduled every 14 days, were a constant reminder of the ticking clock, while the chemotherapy sessions, precisely every 21 days, represented a fierce fight for survival.

I navigated through the sterile white rooms, where conflicting labels of age were placed upon me - too old to bear a child comfortably, yet too young to undergo aggressive cancer treatments. Each corner I turned presented its unique set of challenges, a blend of hope and fear tightly woven together. There is routine, and there is near normal; none of this applied to me. Every corner had its challenges. Every time I sat in the hospital rooms, the doctors' words would resound in my mind.

All my doctor's visits unfortunately became a chaotic symphony of medical intervention and maternal instinct. The doctors had solemnly laid out the difficult choice before me. They had carefully explained the risks of continuing the pregnancy while receiving chemotherapy.

Their well-meaning recommendations to consider termination echoed in my mind, a haunting reminder of the risks that loomed over both me and the precious life growing within me. The tears that welled up in my eyes seemed to mirror the storm raging inside my heart, torn between my well-being and that of the fragile being I carried. The examination room seemed to shrink around me, filled with an air of fear and uncertainty. I constantly questioned my strength and wondered if I had the fortitude to face the arduous journey that lay ahead.

In this peculiar dance between life and potential loss, routine and normalcy became foreign concepts. My blood levels had a mind of their own; they dipped and warranted transfusions or other forms of treatment. My white cells needed boosting, my metabolic panel had gone haywire, and all my enzyme levels were elevated. At times like this, termination as a recourse was severely considered.

Once in a while, I questioned my sanity for clinging on. Sometimes, I realized I wasn't going to make it, especially when I glanced in the mirror and saw how swollen and blue I had become. My eyes were startlingly white in comparison. I was fatigued, despairing, and would break down in tears.

As if on cue, I felt the kick. My baby would kick during such times. I would hold my tummy, feeling a generous kick from within, a reminder that I shouldn't give up hope so easily. Despite the tears and dread, I could not deny my love for the life that was growing inside of me. It was a love that overcame my agony and terror, whispering, "Hold on." Choose life.

I recall a time when I felt extremely bloated, and I noticed the smell of ammonia on my breath. I sat nervously in the doctor's office, my heart racing in my chest. I glanced at the framed medical degrees on the wall, searching for some reassurance, but found none.

The doctor entered with a serious expression; her eyes filled with concern. "Esther, I'm afraid I have some difficult news for you," she began gently. "Your recent tests... show a sign of organ overload and failure."

The words went through my mind like a cruel, twisted melody. My hand instinctively cradled my belly, my thoughts racing. My gaze shifted to the doctor's, filled with determination and a tinge of fear. "My baby?" I managed to whisper.

The doctor's face was grim. "Given the complexity of your case, Esther, we're recommending termination. The risks to you and the baby... they are high. We believe termination would provide the best chance of survival for both of you."

"Do you mean survival for me?"

"Yes," she responded firmly.

My heart sank as tears welled in my eyes. I clung to my unborn child, my strength failing. "No," I said, my voice trembling but resolute. "I won't let go of this precious life inside of me. We'll fight together."

And fight we did. The following days and weeks were filled with hospital visits, pills, chemotherapy sessions, and a series of debilitating side effects. My body weakened, my hair fell into clumps, and my pale skin showed exhaustion. Through it all, I refused to surrender. I delved deep into research, exploring every possible complementary treatment that could offer a glimpse of hope. Some specialists became my guiding light, especially when it came to understanding the significance of nutrition in my battle.

I found comfort in the arms of my loved ones. My friends, family, and fellow survivors became my pillars of strength. Encouraging me when I felt hopeless and lifting me when I stumbled. Their love was a lifeline, giving me hope even on my darkest days. As my belly grew and my body weakened, I discovered a newfound strength within myself. A fierce love for my unborn child pushed me forward, defying the odds and grim predictions. Though overwhelmed by pain and fear, my determination was firm.

Not to blow my own trumpet, but my courageous decision spread among the medical community, inspiring the hearts of those who witnessed my resilience. I chose to become a symbol of hope and an advocate for other pregnant women facing similar circumstances.

During the eventful year of 2021, CBS News embarked on a mission to shed light on a groundbreaking cancer diagnosis affecting women. As fate would have it, my phone rang with a call from my doctor, bearing an unexpected invitation. The doctor's request startled me - an opportunity to be featured in an interview with the renowned news station.

The doctor's voice over the phone was filled with pride and a hint of admiration. They mentioned that the news station was seeking an interviewee among their patients and didn't hesitate to recommend me. "I could think of no one other than you," she declared. Her words echoed in my mind like a mantra of empowerment.

My story was shared, providing support and guidance, particularly to women of color. At that moment, as the credits rolled on the screen, I realized that sometimes, the most courageous decisions are not made for oneself but for the countless others who find hope in the light you carry.

Throughout my journey, I discovered a valuable lesson: never allow fear to control the decisions you make. In the end, after the birth of my precious baby, I triumphantly resumed my chemotherapy sessions. Now, my health stands strong and unwavering. Being the sole boy amidst my three wonderful daughters, I consider myself truly blessed and fortunate to have the honor of cherishing my son throughout my entire life.

Chapter 9: The Battle Within: Depression

MY EXPERIENCE WITH depression was a challenging and deeply personal journey. It all began during a time of unrest in my life, as I found myself carrying a pregnancy while undergoing chemotherapy. Despite the physical and emotional strain, I had a fierce determination to fight for the survival of my baby and our future together.

The overwhelming love and responsibility I felt toward my unborn child gave me strength during those difficult days. However, after the birth of my baby, a profound emptiness settled within me. It was as if all the fight had been drained from my being.

As the adrenaline subsided and the harsh reality of my situation sank in, a whole new struggle emerged. I was caught off guard by the emptiness that followed, like a stealthy thief who snuck in and drained all the vibrancy from my existence. Depression, a merciless tyrant, gripped me tightly with its icy hand, smothering any glimmer of happiness that should have accompanied this fresh chapter of my life. It whispered deceitful tales of worthlessness and hopelessness, casting a dark shadow over everything.

With the baby now taken care of and having to return to the chemotherapy sessions, my vision shifted. My motivation and energy levels dropped, leaving me feeling like a mere shell of my former self. I slipped into denial when the word "depression" was hurled at me, since I always considered myself mentally strong.

"How could I be depressed? Me? Of all the people?" It was a blow to my self-esteem. As my confidence took a hit, I started to wonder whether there could be another way to look at this.

Depression is often misunderstood as simply feeling sad or down, but it goes much further than that. It is a strong force that can engulf every aspect of your life, robbing you of joy, sapping your energy, and distorting your perception of reality. It is a complex mental health condition that impacts millions globally. It's important to recognize that each person's journey with depression is individual. What I've faced may not mirror the struggles of others.

My journey has taught me the significance of recognizing subtle signs. At first, it was just a feeling of being overwhelmed, like an invisible weight pressing down my shoulders. Then, my heart would race for no apparent reason, leaving me feeling exhausted both mentally and physically.

However, perhaps one of the most challenging aspects was the self-doubt that started to kick in. Lack of sleep became a common companion, and the struggle was intensified as I had recently given birth to my son. The demands of caring for him made the whole situation even more difficult.

As I navigated this unfamiliar terrain, I started to observe delicate hints that murmured something deeper was brewing. The smile that did not reach my eyes, the heaviness in my chest that never seemed to lift, the hollow feeling that echoed through my soul. When I first discussed my struggles with my doctor, she suggested, "Perhaps self-care and self-love are the solutions you're seeking."

No matter how hard I tried to follow her advice, it didn't quite provide the solace I longed for. So, I embarked on a journey to discover different ways to take care of myself. This involved indulging in the calming glow of scented candles, enjoying refreshing showers, immersing myself in soothing melodies, and even attempting to uplift my spirits by donning alluring lingerie.

I also reached out to my partner, saying, "Could you possibly give me massages to help with the tension?" While these acts of self-care might be transformative for some, they failed to produce the desired outcomes for me.

Despite the unwavering support from my loved ones, it was disheartening to frequently experience a sense of loneliness. During such moments, an internal voice would lament, "Why am I turning into my own worst enemy?" Then there were times when my anxiety played tricks on me, causing me to doubt the sincerity of those in my life.

I also came across kind-hearted people who, despite their good intentions, unknowingly made my despair worse. "Cheer up," they would advise.

Those two words ignited a chain reaction of negative self-perception, reinforcing my belief that I was incompetent. After all, I could not even hide my troubles adequately! This internal rebuke left me constantly berating myself for not concealing my true feelings, sustaining a relentless cycle of guilt and self-reproach.

As night fell and darkness shrouded the world, the inner voices grew louder, their taunts taking on a more sinister tone. It seemed as if the night had granted them unrestricted power. The peaceful escape of sleep eluded me, intensifying my inner conflict. The combination of insomnia and depression made the enemy appear unconquerable. Every night, I faced a draining struggle, matching exhaustion with despair.

Eventually, feeling at my wit's end, I consulted my doctor again. On this visit, she prescribed sleeping aids and broached the topic of postpartum depression. "Considering you've recently given birth, it might be postpartum depression," she suggested.

As I went through this emotional rollercoaster, engaging with family and friends became very challenging. The fear of being a burden, combined with a lack of energy to socialize, was overwhelming. I felt as though I was living in a bubble of despair, entirely detached from the world around me.

I often found myself lost in a maze of emotions, unable to find my way out. The world felt distant, colors muted, and laughter a sound from a forgotten past. It was a loneliness that suffocated, a sadness that consumed. Each day became a battle, a struggle to exist simply.

Three months later, my emotional state had only worsened. Despite the passage of time, nothing had improved. In fact, it felt as if my situation had deteriorated. I began to question my worth, wondering if perhaps I was indeed a liability to those around me. Even though I recognized the irrationality of these thoughts, they felt tangibly real in my distress.

The mounting bills reminded me of my unemployment status and the rapid depletion of my savings, worsening my emotional state further. I used to ponder, "How do I even put into words the sensation of numbness?" It is quite a challenge to capture this feeling accurately. It is like being ensnared in a state of emotional emptiness, where thoughts and emotions seem to fade away. I found myself mechanically moving through life with a heavy mask, feigning happiness, especially when in the company of friends and family. But, in truth, it was nothing more than a performance, a desperate aim at fitting in. In solitude, this impassiveness seemed to enlarge. I had ceased reading, abandoned my juicing routine, and generally lost all motivation to try or care.

My partner would say to me, "Please try to find 'us' again."

But if he could probe into my thoughts, he'd have heard a silent counter. "How can I when I can't even find myself?"

Then there were the physical changes. The effects of cancer treatment, including hair loss and weight changes, made me question who I was and my true value. Every trip to the doctor's office and the inevitable weigh-in reminded me of the weight I should lose. With time, those visits became something I began to dread and avoid.

My doctor then suggested that what I was going through wasn't just postpartum depression but rather a more complex form of the condition. That conversation was a wake-up call, signaling that my mental well-being needed more comprehensive care than I'd realized. Despite my fatigue, I found strength. "Can I focus less on the chemo and more on treating my depression?" I asked, unsure if I was advocating for myself or merely voicing my weariness. All I knew was that I longed to feel better.

You see, dealing with depression can sometimes make you feel alone. Despite the support from professionals and loved ones, finding the inner strength to cope with such intense emotions is not always easy. Personally, I often found myself doubting if anyone truly grasped the extent of my pain. Their words of encouragement were kind, but I could not help but wonder if they truly comprehended the magnitude of my fight.

There was a scheduled appointment with a psychiatrist. Stepping into the psychiatrist's office for my appointment, I noticed the walls decorated with lively paintings, brightening up the room. The gentle music playing in the background added to the peaceful atmosphere. Despite the calming environment, I could not shake off the feeling of unease. My mind was filled with racing thoughts, making it difficult to know where to begin the conversation. I struggled to fully grasp the doctor's words, often finding myself lost in the sea of his explanations. As much as I tried to understand what he was saying, I often just could not.

As the doctor wrapped up the appointment and gently said, "You're dealing with depression," it felt like time stood still for a moment. The world seemed to move in slow motion. But instead of sinking into despair, a wave of relief washed over me. Finally, I had a name for what I was experiencing. It was no longer a mystery. The doctor assured me that with the right combination of therapy and medication, I could not only cope with these emotions but also regain control over my life.

However, that diagnosis did not mark the end of my fight against depression. It was more like a suffocating cloak, isolating me further. It actually intensified my struggles. Embracing a condition with such a heavy stigma is truly challenging. It is tough.

Then, there was a certain stigma attached to discussing mental health while undergoing cancer treatment. The expectation to appear strong and positive was overwhelming. It was as though admitting to my emotional battles was a betrayal of the facade of resilience I was expected to uphold. The burden of this expectation is simply dismissive of the emotional battles faced by cancer patients, period. I decided to defy societal expectations and make my mental well-being my top priority. Let's not forget that seeking assistance for our mental health is not a sign of weakness but rather a display of strength and resilience.

"Cancer" is a word that strikes fear into the hearts of many. While the physical toll it takes on the body is widely discussed and understood, the emotional toll often remains under the radar. Throughout my cancer treatment, I came face-to-face with the overwhelming emotional rollercoaster that accompanies the disease. From the initial shock of my diagnosis to struggling with thoughts of suicide, I was swirled into a storm of emotions that often seemed unmanageable. Like many others, I had always linked cancer with physical pain, never truly acknowledging the profound impact it might have on my mental well-being.

However, I refused to let stigma dictate my journey. I refused to suppress my truth for the comfort of others. I took a stand for my mental well-being, knowing that it was a crucial component of my overall health. A step towards reclaiming my narrative from the jaws of stigma.

Going through this challenging period has sparked a fire within me to shed light on mental health concerns. I've become a champion for showing kindness and understanding to people dealing with similar struggles. Through sharing my experiences, I aim to motivate others to accept and reach out for assistance without letting fear or embarrassment stop them. Let's work together to build a more compassionate community that stands by those fighting against depression.

Chapter 10: The Treatment Plan

DARK CLOUDS HUNG HEAVILY over my life as I walked into the doctor's room. My body functioned on autopilot as if detached from my true self. The constant struggle with depression had drained me completely. But in that crucial moment, I summoned the strength to open up to the doctor, revealing that I had finally hit rock bottom. Little did I realize that this one confession would ignite a chain of events that would alter the course of my existence forever.

My desperation and the urgency of the situation prompted the doctor to swiftly take action. Realizing the risk I was in, she promptly reached out to my partner and called for an ambulance to guarantee my well-being. My mental condition was so severe that I was deemed a danger to myself and considered to have diminished mental capacity.

I made a grave error by attempting to handle things on my own. One day, while my family was away at work or school and the baby was at daycare, I found myself sitting alone at the dining table. Suddenly, it struck me that there was a solution - to put an end to my life. I must have smirked at this realization. I headed to the kitchen, where I cut my wrists with a knife. However, the pain jolted me back to reality, and I discovered that the blade was dull. Blood was flowing, nevertheless. My only choice was to rush to bed, swallow some sleeping pills, and await my demise.

I must have dozed off due to sheer mental fatigue. Upon regaining consciousness, I found myself questioning what had occurred. Observing my wrist, I realized that the blood flow had ceased; the wound had closed. Despite feeling disappointed, I resolved to seek a better alternative. The next day, I reluctantly attended the chemotherapy session that I had been avoiding. While filling out the questionnaire, I openly admitted to being severely depressed, having suicidal thoughts, and even having a plan. This confession led my oncologist to panic, resulting in the urgent summoning of security and an ambulance.

By this stage of my life, I had already reached out to professionals and started taking antidepressants. I had held onto the hope that these measures would bring me some respite from the constant darkness that enveloped my everyday existence. Yet, deep within the recesses of my mind, a looming shadow persisted, growing heavier with each passing day. It was as if a dark cloud had descended upon my world, painting everything in shades of gray. A tempest raged within me; unlike any storm I had ever encountered. Despite my medication, my anxiety and despair refused to wane, persisting with unwavering determination. The medical community had labeled my condition "treatment-resistant depression," a term that offered little comfort.

Before I knew it, I found myself confined within the sterile walls of a hospital, awaiting transfer to a specialized facility for psychiatric care. The psychiatric facility, with its guarded fences and stringent routines, kept me separated from the outside world. It was both my refuge and my prison, providing a structured environment aimed at healing the fractures in my mind.

This inpatient mental treatment center was a watershed moment for me, I'll admit. It was a welcome diversion that allowed me to concentrate on my health journey while I got the help I needed. I feel compelled to correct the widespread misconception that an inpatient mental institution is some kind of vacation spot or five-star resort. Instead, it is designed to give people a safe space to recover from depression and other mental health issues by providing them with therapy and the support they need.

Getting admitted into the psychiatric ward served as a stark reminder of the seriousness of mental illness. I could not help but feel ashamed that it had reached this point. Having our mouths inspected after each medical session was a wake-up call. Even though battling depression was tough I took solace in the fact that I wasn't facing it alone.

Nevertheless, it's crucial to emphasize that depression should never be downplayed. There is always the heightened feeling of confinement, both mentally and physically. For example, the hospital garbs we had to wear only intensified this feeling of being trapped. The garments served as a constant reminder of our status as patients, each labeled as battling their inner demons. Then there was the unwavering dedication and watchful eye of the devoted staff members.

Despite their care and attention, an underlying sense of fear persisted within me. Witnessing a fellow patient succumb to violence and being forcefully tackled and subdued was a distressing sight that left a lasting impact on me. Since that fateful day, I preferred solitude as I navigated my own emotional battles.

Throughout my time there, I was fortunate enough to be paired with an incredibly quiet lady as my roommate. Our exchanges were few and far between. The lack of familiar faces in that setting served as a powerful reminder of the loneliness that can accompany such an environment. Nevertheless, this encounter granted me a deep insight into the diverse individuals who seek assistance in psychiatric facilities. Despite our vastly different backgrounds, we were able to forge connections and provide mutual support as we embarked on this shared path.

During my time here, there were instances when I deeply yearned for home. The ache of missing my kids and my significant other sometimes became too much to bear. Unfortunately, the strict regulations at the facility meant we could not have cell phones.

Spending a day in a psychiatric ward offers a one-of-a-kind and challenging experience. Your entire day is meticulously planned out, starting from the minute you open your eyes until you drift off to sleep. The daily schedule can feel repetitive at times, with a mix of therapy sessions, group activities, and medication routines.

In a psychiatric ward, each day is carefully crafted to foster stability and recovery. The mornings kick off with the administration of medications, followed by breakfast, before engaging in group therapy sessions. These sessions serve as a platform for patients like me to open up, exchange experiences, acquire valuable coping techniques, and forge meaningful connections.

Afternoons were typically filled with individual therapy sessions, followed by recreational activities and educational programs. With individual therapy sessions, we were guided to delve into the depths of our minds, dissecting our thoughts and emotions with precision.

Following the rigorous sessions, we had the chance to probe into and explore the realm of recreational activities and educational programs. The options were varied, but what caught my attention the most were the alternative methods of healing, such as art therapy and music therapy. These unconventional techniques provided us with a means to convey our emotions that words often fall short of expressing.

Despite the enticing activities, I often found solace in the quiet corners of the library. Surrounded by shelves of books that held a world of knowledge and escape, I would lose myself in the pages, letting the words weave their magic around me. Journaling became my silent confidante, a safe space where my thoughts could flow freely without judgment.

In the beginning, I must confess that my afternoons were spent in a haze of exhaustion, my body craving rest from the emotional turmoil of therapy. My initial days were spent napping, with little motivation to participate in anything beyond the mandatory activities.

In the wards, evenings were dedicated to winding down and practicing self-care. Activities ranged from relaxation exercises, additional journaling, or engaging in quiet activities such as reading or listening to soothing music. We were told that the goal was to create an atmosphere conducive to restful sleep and emotional well-being. We were supposed to get at least eight hours of sleep every night and go to bed at a reasonable hour.

Then, there was the weekly visit to the physician. These visits were mandatory, although not as frequent as I might have desired. Still, they occurred as often as was feasible. I found it very important to be honest and transparent with the doctor during these consultations. These visits were an opportunity to communicate any unpleasant experiences or symptoms encountered during treatment, allowing the medical team to ascertain my well-being.

Although family visits were permitted in the facility, I chose not to encourage them. I did not want my family, especially my partner, to see me in such a vulnerable state. My reluctance also stemmed from the realization that my partner already had a plethora of responsibilities back at home, ranging from dropping the children off at school to managing bedtime routines.

Amidst the gloom and despair that had consumed my life, there was one enchanting experience that brought a glimmer of hope during my stay - the elegant peacocks that graced the facility's grounds. Their vibrant feathers created a striking contrast to the darkness that surrounded me, offering a momentary escape from my troubles. Each time I caught a glimpse of these majestic creatures, my spirits soared as they gracefully danced, providing a much-needed respite from the hardships I faced. These peacocks became my silent companions, bringing a touch of wonder and unexpected joy to my days, reminding me that beauty can be found even in the most unlikely of places.

An alternative approach to healing that was completely unfamiliar to me suddenly emerged as a potential lifeline: Electroconvulsive therapy (ECT). Even though I later learned about ECT's negative stigma and controversial past, I remained optimistic that it could offer relief to individuals battling severe, untreatable depression. At last, there seemed to be a glimmer of hope for those like me who had tried every other available treatment.

The treatment was carried out in accordance with legal regulations, particularly the Mental Capacity Act of 2005 or the Mental Health Act of 1983, since I was unable to provide informed consent, perhaps because I did not fully comprehend the consequences of ECT. The court mandated the intervention.

Little did I know at the time, but it was only after exhausting all other treatment options that I would become eligible for ECT. This is precisely why it is referred to as a last-resort treatment. Stepping into the world of ECT, I experienced a mix of fascination and terror. Despite the unsettling images that come to mind, no one can deny the therapy's remarkable effectiveness in addressing severe and treatment-resistant depression.

As my name was put down on the list for ECT, it was a moment of anticipation tinged with fear, but no glimmer of optimism in that fear, only a sense of uncertainty. It was a moment of whatever happens. My sight had been blurred by a thick fog of depression for far too long.

Certain mental health conditions can be effectively addressed through electroconvulsive therapy, a procedure that induces controlled seizures by administering electrical stimulation to the brain. Studies show that it has helped numerous individuals, although the precise mechanisms behind its effectiveness remain unclear. Despite lingering negative perceptions due to historical misuse, advancements in methodology and a focus on patient well-being have paved the way for a more personalized and safer application of this treatment.

Under closely monitored conditions, I underwent ECT treatments. The process involved electrodes being placed on my scalp, followed by a controlled electrical current. Despite what you may have seen in movies, it wasn't as dramatic as you might think. I would be taken to the treatment room, given a muscle relaxant, and asked some questions to recite my name, date of birth, current date, or similar information. Then, I would wake up in the recovery room. Following a brief period of disorientation, a nurse would assist me to a recliner, from where I would be wheeled back to the facility to recover.

I'll admit my journey with electroconvulsive therapy was far from easy. In the beginning, I could not see any positive changes, not until after my fourth session. It was truly disheartening. However, my doctor assured me that this was just a normal part of the process. Despite the initial lack of progress, I held onto hope and prayed for some signs of improvement. Slowly but surely, as my doctor increased the intensity of the ECT sessions, I started noticing a shift. By the time I completed my sixth treatment, something extraordinary occurred: I began to feel different. The heavy cloud of depression that had consumed me for so long started to dissipate, allowing glimpses of light and hope to shine through.

Following this crucial juncture, I was granted the opportunity to head back home and adhere to a well-structured therapy routine, take my prescribed medication daily, and undergo continuous ECT treatments as an outpatient. I am deeply appreciative of my partner, who made sure to drive me to the facility every fortnight.

Often, I found myself surrounded by fellow ECT patients in the recovery room. Although we did not talk much due to the draining nature of the treatment, the peaceful silence between us was always comforting, never awkward.

Amid the soul-crushing anguish, my life started to turn a corner. "Only God knows," I often found myself whispering in solitary reflection. It was a slow, grueling process, marked by episodes of hospitalization, medication adjustments, and eventually a decision that carried its emotional weight: embarking on electroconvulsive therapy (ECT). Allow me to be painfully honest with you: ECT was not a magical cure for my crippling depression, but it did something profoundly important. It saved my life.

Before undergoing ECT, I was teetering on the brink of existence, inundated with suicidal thoughts and paralyzed by the symptoms of my depression. But after the treatment, I felt as though I had been given a lifeline. I was able to regain my footing, find some semblance of balance, and return to a state that felt much closer to neutral. This was nothing short of a miracle for me.

I'm forever grateful for those early morning procedures that pulled me back from the edge of the pit. While I manage my ongoing depression through medication, I know that if I ever plummet back into that unbearable darkness, ECT may be an option. It was a safety net. I strongly urge you, if you or a loved one are entangled in the brutal vines of depression, to consider ECT as an option. Despite its unsettling name and the lingering societal stigma, its profound impact on my mental well-being has been undeniable.

It is crucial to acknowledge a major downside of ECT: the possibility of experiencing severe memory loss. I am among the numerous individuals who have endured this exhausting side effect. Even at present, I continue to grapple with unsettling gaps in my memory, which I will delve deeper into in the upcoming chapter. No one should have to endure the anguish of memory loss while seeking healing, and yet, unfortunately, this is our reality.

As I wrap up my contemplation, my thoughts irresistibly return to the vivid imagery of the peacocks gracing the grounds of the psychiatric facility. Their stunning, regal display feels like a powerful metaphor for enduring hardship yet emerging with a sense of grace and beauty. Whenever I saw them, my spirits lifted momentarily, as if they whispered a gentle reminder: even in the bleakest situations, there's a space for beauty and a chance for recovery. Living through the dark maze of depression and experiencing the unexpected relief brought on by ECT has shown me the incredible strength and unyielding spirit that lies within us, humans.

Chapter 11: Amnesia

IN THE GENESIS, as "the one with amnesia"—meaning the one with the inability to remember—I had to struggle with a disturbing reality. I could neither form new memories nor retain information, let alone execute daily tasks effectively. To put it bluntly, I was a stranger even to myself. Fragments of my past life were scattered like pieces of an unsolvable puzzle; my story was now lost, disappearing into the dark crevices of my memory.

Throughout the annals of time, people have grappled with the debilitating effects of amnesia, a condition often linked to memory loss stemming from various causes. In my own personal journey, my battle with amnesia began after undergoing Electroconvulsive Therapy (ECT). This treatment was meant to address my mental health issues, but it led to unforeseen repercussions. Over time, I realized that I could no longer recall important milestones in my life, like treasured family trips or the miraculous arrival of my child. Thus, I found myself on a perplexing path, filled with anxiety, uncertainty, and the daunting challenge of piecing together my shattered sense of self.

Every time I found myself on the hospital bed, my body tensed as jolts of electricity surged through me. Despite the pain, my desire for a fresh start motivated me to push through. "It is a small price to pay for a chance at joy once more," I reassured myself eventually. Yet, as I continued with the ECT sessions, it became evident that something was terribly missing.

As I emerged from the depths of depression, I began to realize something disconcerting. Memories that were once etched into my mind now appeared blurry, like elusive fragments of dreams. Worried, I confided in my doctor, desperately seeking answers to make sense of this perplexing situation. The disappearance of ordinary, everyday memories left me feeling bewildered and adrift.

The cherished family vacations that once brought immense happiness to my soul were now an irreplaceable void. The moments of pure joy, the significant milestones, the unforgettable celebrations, and the joyous festivities that were once the essence of my being were slowly fading away, leaving empty gaps in my memories. However, what truly shook me to my very core was the devastating realization that the precious memory of my son's birth had vanished without a trace.

The weight of losing such precious moments overwhelmed me, and I desperately sought answers. I vividly recall confiding in my doctor about my concerns. With empathy in her voice, she reassured me, "Your memory loss is likely temporary." She went on to explain, "The brain sometimes employs forgetting as a defense mechanism, shielding itself from recalling traumatic events or the distressing emotions associated with those experiences."

I inquired about the condition, "What do you call this?"

"It is referred to as retrograde amnesia," she responded. "It often impacts memories around the time of the ECT sessions. However, in certain instances, this memory loss can extend back several months or even years. Unfortunately, you fall into that latter group."

I inquired with curiosity, "And what about chemotherapy?"

"Keep in mind that chemotherapy can also cause memory issues of its own," she replied.

Every visit to the doctor seemed to only deepen my bewilderment. The complex medical terms, such as "retrograde amnesia," had started to feel like everyday vocabulary in our discussions. It felt like we were running out of words to describe my condition, yet my desire to regain my lost memories remained unfulfilled. Not only did important memories slip away from me, but even basic directions to the nearby grocery store escaped my memory, along with the identities of familiar faces and names. What used to be a simple act of stepping outdoors now felt like a challenging feat.

Consequently, I found myself heavily dependent on others for guidance and support, leaving me with a sense of unease. It was quite unsettling to discover myself in such a predicament. While seeking treatment for depression should typically lead to an improvement in overall well-being, this newfound anxiety seemed counterintuitive. Internally, I questioned why this unexpected outcome was occurring, struggling to connect the dots.

In a remarkably clear incident, my partner and I had organized a trip to Mexico. Unfortunately, they were unable to travel on the planned day due to unforeseen circumstances. This unexpected twist of fate left me feeling anxious as I pondered on the next steps, particularly when it came to arranging transportation from the airport to our hotel.

With a nervous tone, I turned to my 18-year-old and asked, "Are you capable of driving?" The desperation in my voice was unmistakable.

"Absolutely, I can take care of it," she reassured me, stepping up to face the challenge.

To my surprise, she skillfully navigated the rental car through unfamiliar roads with astonishing ease. It was truly impressive. While I felt relieved, a hint of embarrassment also crept in. That day, I made a strong decision to halt any future ECT treatments.

The impact of my memory loss had now started to affect my relationships with my family, causing painful reminders during our interactions. Memories that used to flow effortlessly were now mere fragments slipping away from my grasp like sand slipping through clenched fists. Daily routines, conversations, and even promises I had made were a struggle to recall. Living with a poor memory had become an exasperating part of my everyday life.

"Mom, do you remember when we went to that restaurant?" my child would ask, hoping for a shared memory.

"Or the day you helped me move into my college dorm?" they would add, seeking a connection.

Every time, my response remained the same: filled with regret. "I'm sorry, honey, I can't recall," I would admit, feeling my heart sink as I acknowledged the weight of my memory's absence.

The most treasured memories were now buried in the labyrinth of my mind. With time, I had come to understand that those direct questions were not accusations but sincere efforts from my family to help me reclaim my lost memories. Nevertheless, the burden weighed heavily on me.

Following a period of self-reflection in Mexico, I was determined to move forward and reconstruct my life, regardless of the memory loss. At the forefront of my goals was getting back into the workforce. With pregnancy behind me, depression under control, and chemotherapy treatments scheduled every three weeks, I was eager to kickstart my professional journey once again.

"My advice? Resume your life exactly where you left off before all these medical complications," said Jordan, my kind-hearted therapist, during one of our sessions. She believed wholeheartedly in the healing power of normalcy.

Prior to my health issues, I worked as a drug safety veterinarian in the corporate world, a role that brought me immense satisfaction. However, the idea of going back to that position seemed daunting. It wasn't just about relearning my job duties; job interviews triggered a new kind of anxiety that I had never experienced before.

"So, you're suggesting that I should simply jump back into my career?" I inquired cautiously, my hands tightening.

"Yes," she confirmed, "Sometimes the only way to remember how to swim is to dive back into the water."

Despite her uplifting encouragement, the fear I felt remained lingering in the depths of my being. It was as if my entire world had transformed into a grand stage, where everyone else effortlessly recited their lines while I stood there, my own forgotten.

In between therapy sessions—both chemo and cognitive—I reached out to my former employer to inquire about possible job openings. They promptly redirected me to the disability company. This set off a dispiriting back-and-forth between the two entities. Undeterred, I took matters into my own hands and began applying for various positions on the company's website, aiming to rebuild my life. What I did not realize was that I was venturing into turbulent waters without a guiding compass.

Job interviews used to be a breeze, but now they're nothing short of anxiety-inducing. Every time I sit down with my resume in hand, I struggle to recall my achievements and strengths. The memory of my first job interview post-amnesia still haunts me. I held onto a freshly printed resume that felt like it belonged to someone else.

"So, Ms. Wafula, can you share details about the most challenging project you've managed" the interviewer inquired.

I was at a loss for words. My mind went blank as I tried to come up with a response. My past experiences seemed like distant memories that were impossible to access. Their gaze bore into me, waiting for an answer. The room felt suffocating, and my confidence wavered. All I could feel were clammy hands and blurred vision.

Gathering my courage, I mustered the strength to speak up. "Sir," I began, momentarily closing my eyes as my mind went blank again. "I apologize for my hesitation, but I have to be honest with you."

With that, I opened up about my ongoing recovery from amnesia and described it as the most complex project I had ever tackled. I did not get the job that day, and many more rejections would follow. Nonetheless, each interview was another step in the complicated journey of rediscovering me.

Witnessing potential job opportunities slip away due to my inability to recall crucial details was an incredibly frustrating experience. The confidence I once had seemed like a distant memory, leaving me grappling with the fear of being exposed as someone with an impaired memory.

One bright, crisp morning, I had what I thought was a promising job interview. I had been here once—this was my former hive, where I was once a trusted worker. Now, I was a humble bee seeking re-entry into this buzzing world. It was the exact position I had once held—the one I had been told I duly merited. I was elevated to cloud nine, and the buoyant vibe started to encircle me once again.

As I stepped into the interview room, my heart did a flip. There they were—familiar faces looking back at me. My former colleagues, some of whom I had personally interviewed and vouched for. The situation's awkwardness filled the room with a silence so loud it could dull a roar. As I looked around, I saw faces that were familiar yet uncertain.

We conversed—awkward small talk peppered with subtle hints of uncertainty and questions I had once employed to assess potential. As the interview progressed, the expressions on the faces of my interviewers painted a bleak picture. Their solicitous smiles offered no comfort; their eyes mirrored a dilemma caught between past camaraderie and present obligations. Despite my qualifications and experience, my employer—having previously given me time off—was not in a position to rehire me. My expectations were shattered as their words hit me like icy stones, leaving me feeling utterly deflated and my confidence in tatters.

In despair, I canceled all my other applications with this company. Yet, through all this, I gained something far more precious: acceptance of my new identity and a tremendous source of courage. From this experience, I realized that life's cycles are entanglements of happiness, despair, and the in-betweens. Sometimes, we're the judges; other times, we're judged. Either way, the journey continues as we swim against the currents of destiny.

So, I walked away, not with a tinge of bitterness but with a heart full of acceptance and hope. I was ready for my next journey—another hive, perhaps, another colony—where I might find my worth again.

Indeed, amnesia shook the ground beneath me, casting doubt on my capabilities, but it could not prevent me from soaring high. It was a challenge but also a catalyst that led me down a path of self-discovery and courage. Each day is and continues to be, a step ahead in retrieving my lost story, one puzzle piece at a time.

Afraid, I was. Insecure, yes. Every day was a relentless struggle, a predictable chaos. Each sunrise posed a question, and each sunset became an unfulfilled plea. But above all else, it became an exploration, an expedition. I was my isolated island, my own intricately spinning globe, and my skilled geographer. Amid this loss, I found an ironic gift: a chance to know myself again, to unveil the mysteries of a life once lived, and to relive moments from an untouched perspective.

Amnesia is such an unpredictable bedfellow. It robbed me of my past yet left me with fragmented memories, just enough to fuel a sense of loss. Despite making strides in my recovery, traces of amnesia still linger. To this day, the most peculiar part of my condition is the mis-association syndrome. My brain easily confuses left with right and jumbles up numbers, turning the world into a cryptogram. A simple "turn right" from my GPS leads me in the opposite direction. Even a glance at 687 on a screen turns into 678 in my mind.

"676, or is it 767?" I found myself wondering as I stared at a phone number or my old diary. I mentally rearranged the digits in various permutations, determined not to let this quirk of my misfiring neurons plague me anymore. Occasionally, I still stumble, mixing up words, a constant reminder of how this condition affects my cognitive abilities. It is like saying "male" instead of "female." Welcome to my world, where laughter and frustration intertwine in a realm of amusing blunders.

One day, upon my arrival at the therapy clinic, I discovered Jordan seated on the floor, surrounded by a variety of objects. "Esther," she exclaimed with a sparkle in her eyes, "I have a new idea for us to try today."

She had created a small maze using the clinic's furniture, complete with numbered cards placed around it. "I want you to navigate through this maze by following a specific sequence of numbers and turns that I will provide."

Intrigued and slightly puzzled, I agreed to the challenge. Jordan began to give me the instructions, but my mind, as usual, tried to twist the directions. A "587 and a turn right" somehow turned into a "578 and a turn left." Lost in my confusion, I tripped and accidentally knocked over a chair.

Jordan gave me an understanding smile. "It is okay, Esther, let's take it slow. Remember, we don't have a deadline to beat."

"I do have one," I retorted in my mind.

One evening, my daughter was working on her school's science project, something about constellations. As I helped her, she handed me a sheet numbered "123." Instinctively, my mind switched it to "132." But to my astonishment, when I pointed it out, she laughed.

"That's fine, Mummy! Constellations can also be read in multiple ways, just like your numbers!"

Overwhelmed with surprise, I rose to my feet and embraced her tightly. Tears cascaded down my face, unable to contain my emotions. In that very instant, the profound words of an eight-year-old pierced through my heart, forever altering my perspective. It was a pivotal moment that taught me an immeasurable lesson: the importance of granting myself grace: Just like constellations, life can be read in multiple ways. If I make a right instead of a left, I'll still find my way back. Despite the struggles brought on by my amnesia and word mix-ups, they serve as a constant reminder that challenges can lead to new opportunities.

I refused to let these setbacks deter me. Instead, I drew strength from the progress I had made and remained determined to continue rebuilding myself. Life wasn't about the memories I'd forgotten but about the moments I lived. Through pain and loss, I had learned to find joy in each moment and each conversation and looked forward to building new memories while cherishing the fragile remnants of the old ones. The journey had been daunting and sprinkled with disappointments, but each memory fondly recollected and reshared, however inconsistent, had become a rock to cling to in my ocean of forgetfulness.

I would learn that overcoming amnesia is not just about memory recovery; it is about reconstructing one's identity and boosting self-assurance. Exploring new hobbies, following personal passions, and nurturing relationships have played a crucial role in my journey toward finding purpose and fulfillment. Every achievement, no matter how small, contributes to my growing confidence and acceptance of the person I am evolving into.

Amid this loss, I found a chance to know myself again, to unveil the mysteries of a life once lived, and to relive the moments from an untouched perspective. I searched through the missing pieces of myself from the books I had read, the words I had written, the family I had raised, and the love I had shared. It was a journey of losing memories and finding myself. My battleground was within, and I was both the knight and the dragon. As much as I was the night, I was also the dawn. And, every dawn, I found me, tomorrow's yet-to-be.

Yes, my mind might have been affected by amnesia. But I realized I was not solely a tapestry of memories. I wasn't just built from the past; I was also built from the present—the momentum, the journey, the dream. As long as I breathed, I was more than the missing pieces in a puzzle—more than the places I did not remember.

I will conclude by saying this: My struggle with amnesia has pushed me in ways I never imagined. The loss of memories, the challenges in daily life, and the journey of recovery have been demanding, emotionally draining, and, at times, seemingly too insurmountable. By acknowledging my limitations and embracing the support and resources available to me, I have made significant progress in rebuilding myself and forging a new path forward. Amnesia may have caused me to lose parts of my past, but it has also opened doors to newfound strength and fortitude that I will carry with me in the face of any future challenges.

Chapter 12: Recovery

IN THE LAND OF DREAMS and opportunities, with less than ten dollars in my pocket and a family of three eager children, I set foot as a wide-eyed immigrant. With dreams bigger than my fears, I held onto the American Dream—a vision of life filled with peace, prosperity, and boundless potential.

Life went on; days turned into years, and I diligently inched toward my aspirations. However, an unexpected blow fell. The word "cancer," which roils with odious implications, suddenly became my reality. It was as if the bright American sun had been forcibly shrouded in the lonely shadows of despair.

Life sometimes throws tragedies at us in sprints and leaps, and often, we're just left struggling, wondering why fate had to be so cruel. The harsh symphony of life was something I'd come to understand on an excruciatingly intimate journey. Before life saw fit to paint my portrait with the color of blood, I was an everyday woman—healthy, working a 9-to-5 job, shopping, dining out, traveling—caught up in the minutiae of life that most take for granted.

Then came the cancer diagnosis, an intrusive interloper disrupting my well-laid plans. I had anticipated challenges as an immigrant—a linguistic barrier, cultural differences, or racial biases—but not a battle within my own body. Once vibrant, the image in the mirror had now turned into a pale shadow, its strength diminishing. The complexity of my illness did not just affect my body; it brought a jolt to my life, instilling fear, confusion, and hopelessness. I had been crafting an empire designed to offer my children a life that was always out of my grasp as a child. I'd just hit gold: an excellent corporate position, my net worth skyrocketing, and my outstanding physical health. Life was good. I was living in the fast lane, having fought to elevate myself from nothingness to everything. But then came the shock.

I immediately wore a perfume called Denial. "Cancer can't touch me." I thought this denial had its deceit; it smelled of fear, bottled with bravado. "It is a memorable blip, nothing more," I comforted myself. "Surely doctors make mistakes too!" I cloaked myself in impenetrable armor, refusing to let reality seep in.

The truth felt strange. Absurd, even. Was I the protagonist of a Kafkaesque tale who morphed overnight into a cancer patient? I wondered. Denial, they say, is the first stage of grief. Yet denial provided a comforting shelter. It was easier to dismiss the diagnosis as a lie than to accept my all-consuming fear.

But denial, however sturdily crafted, was quicksand, pulling me into a sea of anxiety. It was just a temporary refuge, a paper fort that was fast collapsing under the weight of reality. When finally, the life-corroding words called cancer embedded into my consciousness, it felt like a maelstrom had whirlpooled into my heart's serenity.

"I'm sorry, Esther. The test results indicate a positive..." my doctor's voice began before it faded in my denial. A pit formed in my stomach, and questions gnawed at my heart. "What about my children? What about their future, my legacy?" Fear raced through my mind as my dreams of ensuring an unruffled life for them seemed to teeter on the precipice of an unthinkable abyss.

In those shifting sands of despair, a symphony of survival was born. Such was the song of my life. It all began in 2019, the year the world stopped spinning, and my existence felt suspended between twilight and the darkest night. Finally, after weeks of evasion, I made the hardest decision. I leaped. The surgery was scheduled, and a sense of calm descended upon me as I signed the consent forms. There was no turning back now. As the surgical team wheeled me into the operating room, the sterile smell of the room suffocated my senses, and my heartbeat seemed to echo the surreal reality.

"I'm fighting cancer," I thought to myself, trying to grasp the gravity of the situation as I lay there, waiting for the anesthesia to take effect.

Post-surgery was the beginning of a challenging journey. I had to start radiation therapy. Expecting a steely, cold space similar to a sci-fi movie scene, I was pleasantly surprised to find a comforting, calm environment. Through countless rounds of radiation, I actually got to know the staff. The radiographers and medical physicists became my confidants and friends. Their caring self, technical expertise, and reassuring words became the buoy I clung to in turbulent waters. It was in them that I found my hope, dressed like a scientist.

Radiation was followed by chemotherapy. If radiation was a test of physical endurance, chemotherapy would be the battleground of the spirit. Administered over several sessions, the drugs felt like an alien invasion in my body, causing nausea, fatigue, and hair loss.

At the height of my solitude, I could almost envision myself as a lone warrior on an arduous odyssey. "Each session of chemotherapy is a mythical beast I have to vanquish before moving on to the next one," I told myself, bracing for the battle ahead.

Then came two life-altering events that threw my world into chaos: I had been diagnosed with cancer, and I found out that I was pregnant. The joys of impending motherhood were immediately undercut by panic and uncertainty. "My plans, my dreams—they're all oozing into the abyss," I thought in that fleeting moment.

The doctors, broaching the subject of termination, said chemotherapy could potentially harm the fetus. I found myself wrestling internally, torn between the maternal instinct to protect my unborn child and the instinct to survive. I was in a twirling vortex of uncertainty and fear. "Can I undergo chemotherapy while pregnant?"

After several sleepless nights and endless tears, I decided to seek a second opinion. Hence, I made a tough decision: I would carry my baby and battle cancer at the same time. Though hopeful, I was cast headlong into the ordeal of chemotherapy. My body turned into a battleground, overwhelmed by waves of sickness and exhaustion. Clumps of hair fell out, and a metallic flavor seemed to permanently reside in my mouth. With every passing day, my health dwindled, leaving me weak, fragile, and afraid.

As the delicate life within me grew, the life around me seemed to wither; COVID-19 had struck. The once-vibrant hospital corridors now echoed a chilling emptiness. COVID-19 had spread its monstrous wings, its virulent darkness swallowing everything in its path. The world had come to an abrupt standstill, as if holding its breath, mirroring the stillness within me.

Doctors' visits transformed into sterile encounters. The reassuring humanness of touch dissolved into latex-gloved interactions. Visits behind facemasks and the backdrop of video calls stripped me of the comfort of human connection. I was a warrior without her tribe, navigating an unknown landscape. The fear of death, an insidious stranger, became my constant companion; its grim whispers were an appalling lullaby that wrestled me into sleepless nights.

But within me thrived a small heartbeat, a persistent rhythm that dared to defy exterior upheavals. My unborn child, a beacon of hope in a sea of despair, was a reminder of the incredible duality of life. An oasis at the edge of the desert of desolation. I held on tightly, endlessly tuning into his gentle kicks—as if each one was a whisper saying, "Fight, mama."

During chemotherapy sessions, I kept my hand resting on the swelling promise of life beneath my heart. With every drop of the potent, life-saving poison trickling into me, I locked my gaze on the ultrasound of my unborn child. The image of his tiny form was my compass through the stormy sea of uncertainty. Life was birthing within me, even as the same vessel was being poisoned to purge the disease.

As COVID-19 swept through the land, ravaging everything in its path, I was confined within my home. Unexpectedly, solace came from the distant, collective sounds of human resilience. The once-terrifying world transformed into a canvas of compassion and hope, vibrantly painted by the faraway applause for healthcare workers. My loneliness dissolved into a feeling of universal camaraderie—we were all warriors, fighting our battles, protecting our loved ones, and clinging desperately to hope.

Trapped in this new reality, depression slowly crept in. The routine of my life turned into a mundane existence devoid of the joy and happiness that once colored my days.

Balancing work and health would have been an arduous task, so I was on long-term disability. The financial stress, coupled with the physical pain of my condition, wounded my spirit deeply. My home, once a sanctuary that was lively and warm, now felt as cold and lonely as an icy landscape.

The little heartbeat growing within me remained my pillar of strength through it all. "You and I, little one, we're a team," I would often whisper, my hand cradling my growing belly. He was my solace and my beacon of hope in the stormy sea of my life. As difficult as the journey was, I held onto the comforting thought that I was fighting for not just one life but two.

After what felt like a lifetime of heartache, I delivered a healthy baby boy. "He's perfect," said the nurse as she handed him to me. His tiny fingers curling around my own were the affirmation of life and love I so desperately needed. I held him close, my heart echoing his triumphant cry. It was a victory cry, a defiance against despair. At that moment, I was reminded again I was not just a patient but a mother, a warrior, and a survivor. His innocent eyes filled with life and hope, mirroring mine years before this ordeal - before I was thrown into this unrelenting storm.

After the various medical interventions, I started experiencing memory loss, a side effect I was not prepared for. "Do you remember any of this?" my husband would ask, showing me photos or talking about recent events. Piecing together fragments of recent events felt like attempting a monumental puzzle with missing pieces. "Some days, it is all a blur," I confessed. Life passed hurriedly, leaving blank spaces in my cluttered mind.

Yes, my life had been drenched with the climax of a tragedy. But as I gazed upon my son, his tiny hand gripping my finger, I knew that every storm, every nightmare, had brought me to this moment.

As days drew into weeks, the challenges intensified. Cancer and chemotherapy were not just medical terms; they were my reality. I began to come to terms with the fact that this fight wasn't about brute strength or insight. It was a thorny path, and cancer was an adversary I was unfamiliar with. Yet, it came with collateral beauty—a realization of my vulnerability and my mortality. It forced me to dig deep, not into a vault of tangible assets but into my emotional trench.

I must admit, amidst the gloom, not everything was bleak. After the storm had run its course, I discovered deep reservoirs of strength within me, which I tapped to rise above this adversity. "You can do this," I whispered to myself, clutching the hospital blanket. "You're stronger than you think."

This story is not just about my physical recovery from cancer; it is also about my journey of rediscovery, the lessons imbibed, and my unwavering hope in the American Dream—even in the face of tumult.

Being an immigrant, the American Dream has served as a shining light of hope for me, steering me towards a successful career, a comfortable home, and a sense of belonging. The pursuit of these dreams while battling cancer was like traveling through a difficult mountain. The climb was steep, the path was rocky, and most of the time, the peak was covered with uncertainty.

Going through treatments and dealing with the dreadful side effects, one thing that remained constant was the American healthcare system. Yes, the oncologists, nurses, and even the janitors at the hospital became my true companions. They reminded me that the journey wasn't about the ailment alone but also about the astounding mobilization of resources and individuals dedicated to preserving life - a tableau of the American Dream in its altruistic form.

Secondly, cancer gave me an unusual gift: it transformed me from a mere participant in the American Dream to an experiential learner. Amid sleepless nights and painful chemotherapy sessions, I dissected this dream. Was it just a materialistic goal, or did it encompass something broader? Was it merely a personal endeavor, or did it involve nurturing relationships and fostering social bonds?

As I ventured deeper, my perspective evolved, broadening the parameters of this dream. Slowly, survival became less about hanging on to life and more about appreciating the brighter side of it. "Keep up the good fight," a nurse would often tell me, her voice cheerful despite the gravity of the situation.

Every time the nursing staff greeted me with such cheer, every time fellow patients offered words of comfort, and every time my doctor reassured me with a soft pat on the back, I experienced the humanity deeply rooted in American society— another facet of the American Dream that I had early on, not been able to fully see.

Ironically, the dread and pain that filled my world brought forth resilience and grit. The ordeal made me witness first-hand the true essence of the human spirit during the bleakest times. That, in essence, was the modified version of the American Dream in my life—showing kindness and receiving it, fighting hardships while maintaining hope, and serving the community despite personal tribulations.

Then, slowly but surely, the lines on my medical report started looking less intimidating and less ominous. I could distinctly see a streak of dawn at the end of a long, starless night. The torment of chemotherapy gradually disappeared as I became stronger, defiant, and almost unbeatable. This personal hell I had been thrown into galvanized my spirit and crystallized a grain of truth——I was more resilient than I ever knew.

After several arduous months, I heard the words I'd been longing to hear! The sun had just begun to peek through the curtains as I slowly opened my eyes. It had been three long years on this journey. Today was the day I had been waiting for – my final check-up after a long, tiresome battle with cancer. As I stepped into the hospital, memories flooded back. The chemotherapy, the surgeries, and the countless days and nights spent feeling overwhelmed and scared. But today, I felt a glimmer of hope.

Dr. Khaled welcomed me with a friendly smile. I instantly felt a wave of comfort wash over me in her company. As we entered her office, she delved into the details of my recent scans. She talked about tumor markers, hormonal therapies for women under 50 after chemotherapy, and the potential side effects. Despite my efforts to concentrate on her explanations, my mind was preoccupied. My heart raced with anticipation, unable to fully absorb the information she was sharing.

At long last, after what seemed like an endless wait, Dr. Khaled lifted her gaze and delivered the most amazing news, "Esther, I have some extraordinary updates. Your scans show no signs of cancer. You're officially in remission." With a comforting smile, my oncologist shared this heartwarming news.

I could not stop thanking the doctor as tears of relief flowed down my cheeks. It was a whirlwind of emotions - pure happiness and astonishment. Finally, after all the doubts, obstacles, and anxiety, I could finally relax and take a deep breath. Such simple words, yet they carried the weight of my victory, the reward for my relentless fight. After a difficult battle, the day of my remission announcement was here! The brightest dawn was dancing over the horizons of my life. I emerged on the other side, scarred yet radiant, seasoned by the trials of life. This physical healing was important and symbolic. I was victorious; I had survived.

As my family celebrated this news, in my eyes, I saw them as true warriors - their unwavering love and unwavering support during my hardships. They had become my rock, always there to hold me up when I felt like crumbling.

As I walked out of the hospital that day, my mind was filled with thoughts about the incredible journey I had just experienced. Cancer had pushed me to my limits, both physically and emotionally, but it had also revealed a strength within me that I never knew existed. It opened my eyes to the beauty of life and completely transformed my outlook in ways I could never have imagined.

As I embarked on my journey, I discovered solace in the simplest of pleasures - strolling through the park, basking in the gentle caress of the sun on my skin, and treasuring every precious moment. Cancer had bestowed upon me the ability to uncover beauty in the mundane and savor each day as a precious present. With the passage of time, the overwhelming fear that once gripped me gradually dissipated.

The corporate world, which had held immense allure for me before, now seemed insignificant compared to the magnificence of life. I had found a new appreciation for life and health. Cancer, the demon I had conquered, had inadvertently made me a better version of myself.

"What we are in life," I thought to myself, with a newfound sense of gravity, "Is largely dependent on our experiences. Every challenge, every sorrow, and every joy has sculpted me into who I am today."

The lens through which I looked at my world had shifted—irrevocably altered by my battle with this life-altering disease. I had walked the harrowing path of cancer, each step weighed down by the heaviness of denial, pierced by the sharp stabs of fear, and shadowed by the loneliness of solitude. Yet, here I stood, a survivor—I emerged not just victorious but transformed.

Reflecting on my past, the path I've traveled from being an immigrant to overcoming cancer was punctuated with peaks and valleys, each adding a distinctive flavor to my life. Battling against cancer served as a testament to my determination and the collective unity of the nation I now proudly consider my own. The American Dream, once a tangible entity, evolved into a state of mind, a feeling, and a lesson of strength, endurance, and hope.

Indeed, cancer had been a brutal usurper in my life. Yet, paradoxically, it presented an opportunity to delve deep into myself, my dreams, and the core of the country I had chosen to be a part of. Strangely, it refined my American Dream, polishing it into a beacon that not only illuminates my path but also casts a radiating glow on those around me.

As I healed emotionally, fear was replaced by hope, loss by gain, and despair by resilience. Every step I took, every battle I fought, and every hardship I embraced eventually led to a rebirth—the birth of a survivor, a compassionate woman, a participant in a dream that is as diverse as its dreamers, and a proud citizen of the land of opportunity: America. Above all, I learned to be patient with myself.

"As a mother, I can tell you this." I found myself reflecting with a sense of profound insight. "I am not merely a survivor or a mom. I am a woman who found the strength to weather the darkest storms of life and still retain the capacity to love."

While my journey may not be one for the storybooks, it is one painted by resilience, a lesson in hope, and, above all else, a testament to a mother's love. Despite it all, I would not change a thing. Life has been hard, and I admit it continues to be so. But I stand today not despite the pain but because of it.

"I see my son's eyes." My thoughts dwell on the center of my universe, "My world, a world that has seen it all yet looks toward the future—a future that may be uncertain but is still hopeful. I'll repeat. I would not change a thing for life."

You see, after being shackled by the monster called cancer and enduring immense uncertainty, I discovered a new identity—that of a survivor with a resilient spirit. I might not have known how long I'd last in this battle, but what mattered was that my journey itself had become my legacy. My children saw a mom not weakened by disease but powered by will.

For the first time, instead of living life in the fast lane, I learned to stop, to understand, and to cherish the journey, not the destination. I have prioritized my mental health. I have learned to engage in activities that bring joy and relaxation, as well as mindfulness exercises to promote my emotional well-being.

Within this turmoil, I discovered another side to it—one that reminded me of human invincibility, the power to rise even from the ashes. It wasn't about amassing wealth or ensuring a financially secure future for my children; it was about teaching them real values—strength, bravery, and the journey of life—lessons no business deal could have ever offered.

The fight against cancer was not a single-combat war but rather a complex game of chess. It involved a personal struggle that required me to confront my denial, acceptance, and adjustment to the situation. Dealing with the range of emotions that came with it was overwhelming, and I could not have coped alone. Emotionally healing myself has been a critical aspect of my recovery journey.

Support from my loved ones, support groups, and therapy or counseling sessions provided me with an outlet and solace. Wrestling with this new normal brought not only the fear of leaving my children prematurely but also a newfound promise of a legacy that wasn't material.

I have learned many things: to reinvent my dreams, to reimagine my legacy, and to adapt to change. For now, my American Dream bears a new meaning: to leave a legacy of strength and resilience that truly echoes, "Life is not about waiting for the storm to pass; it is about learning to dance in the rain!"

As I end this chapter, this is the ballad of my life. The melody may have been discordant, and the rhythm may have been broken. But it is my song, written with resilience and sung with survival.

Chapter 13: Rebuilding My Life

BEING ON DISABILITY is not easy. The burdens are manifold: the persistent shadow of illness, familial responsibilities, societal expectations, and the ever-looming financial hurdles. Navigating these challenges can be difficult. However, amidst this gloom, a ray of hope persistently shone for me.

I had been living in a state of anxious anticipation leading up to my final chemotherapy session. My doctor had assured me that this was to be my last dance with the chemicals that had been my constant for months.

The hospital room, in its characteristic sterility, was a mix of harsh whites and cold blues. The ever-present antiseptic smell lightly tinged the air. Into this space, the nurse walked in, her demeanor gentle. The kindness in her eyes, a reflection of the empathy and understanding I had witnessed throughout my treatment. "Ms. Wafula," she began, her voice soft, "How do you feel? This is your last session!"

I was overwhelmed with emotions. Tears pooled in my eyes—a mix of relief, joy, and deep-seated gratitude. Grasping for words amidst this torrent of feelings, I managed to say a simple "Thank you" as the familiar sensation of the chemo drugs seeped into my system.

There were phases of doubt, periods where my spirit wavered, wondering if I could shoulder the burdens of this relentless treatment. But the support of my loved ones, the unwavering commitment of my medical caregivers, and my resilience reminded me I had weathered the storm. I had made it. Finally, the last drop of medication emptied into my system, marking the end of my chemotherapy journey. I allowed myself a moment to breathe, to soak in the significance of this milestone. Rising from the chair, a renewed sense of life flowed through my veins as I exited the hospital room.

The sun greeted me, wrapping me in its warm embrace. Its rays cast a golden glow on everything, illuminating the world in a way I hadn't perceived in what felt like forever. Tears, borne not from pain but from profound gratitude, streamed down my face. It was a silent thank you to the universe for granting me another chance to bask in life's myriad wonders.

No longer tethered to the confines of a hospital room, I indulged in the simple, often overlooked pleasures I had missed. The caress of a breeze sifting through leaves, the infectious laughter of children in a park, the riot of colors from blossoming flowers — every fleeting moment felt like a priceless treasure.

With each step I took, it felt as if I was shedding the weight that had anchored me for so long, gradually replacing it with a sense of liberation and endless possibilities.

As the process of rebuilding my life began, I was acutely aware of the impending challenges. I had a successful career before the diagnosis. Now, after remission and facing diminishing finances, I knew I needed a job. Pursuing this was not easy, given my circumstances. With hope, I began sending out applications and waited, eager for responses. But as days turned into weeks and weeks into months, the reality became clear: securing a suitable job was proving to be a great challenge. I poured in my heart and soul with every application, tailoring my resume and cover letter to emphasize my skills and experiences. I also highlighted the profound lessons I learned throughout my career. This dedication bore fruit in the form of a few interviews. However, the lingering amnesia from my illness presented persistent hurdles. In the midst of these interviews, I would often find myself struggling with sudden confusion and memory blanks. These lapses made it difficult to answer questions or recollect vital details.

Despite my attempts to communicate the origins of my condition, many potential employers simply could not see past it, opting for other candidates. In a bid to find a solution, I turned to my former employer. I hoped that they, recognizing a loyal employee who had encountered difficult times, would offer some assistance. But each approach was met with rejection. It dawned on me, with a heavy heart, that the position I once held dear was now beyond my grasp. I had nurtured a hope of rejoining, of being reintegrated into a familiar role. But that was not the reality.

Further adding to my troubles was the changed attitude of my former colleagues. The lively exchanges of the past were now replaced with conversations that felt forced and artificially polite. With this renewed clarity and an unyielding spirit, I shifted my focus. I ventured out, no longer tied to the idea of returning to my previous company, exploring opportunities in diverse organizations.

From my perspective, it is undeniable that individuals who have overcome cancer frequently face a significant transformation in their sense of self and experience challenging emotional adjustments. However, the unjust prejudice associated with being a cancer survivor can intensify feelings of being undervalued and socially isolated. Consequently, this exacerbates the challenges of reintegrating into the workforce, leaving them longing and practically pleading for greater empathy and support from their employers.

Despite the disappointment and deep betrayal from my employer, this experience, as trying as it was, taught me value. It was a reminder of the incredible impact a genuine connection with colleagues can have on one's mental and emotional well-being. In retrospect, this difficult chapter of my life acted as a catalyst, pushing me towards positive change. It urged me to hunt for a more nurturing and understanding work environment, which, in the end, manifested itself as a blessing in disguise.

Furthermore, the employment landscape has transformed, especially following the pandemic. Companies were rapidly shifting towards hybrid work models, while remote work was becoming increasingly popular. Virtual meetings have replaced in-person gatherings, indicating the widespread acceptance of this innovative approach to conducting business. The landscape had changed. I understood the importance of adapting to this new environment in order to secure a position in the job market. Thus, with renewed vigor, I refined my strategy. I tailored my applications not just to spotlight my professional achievements but also to underscore my adaptability and aptitude for thriving in a remote work environment.

During this time, there was a persistent job agency that believed I was a perfect fit for a particular role at a mid-sized Biopharma firm. Yet, a glance at the job description sent a shiver of apprehension down my spine. I was in doubt, making me question if my skills were adequate. We coordinated a time to confer, and the recruiter began, "The pharmaceutical company has conducted several interviews already, but they haven't found the right candidate."

Although trepidation gnawed at me, I conceded, "Alright, I'll give it a shot." After all, I had nothing to lose. The enticing salary was an added incentive. This role was a potential gateway back into the workforce. With determination, I delved deep into preparation – researching the company in-depth, poring over possible interview questions, and diligently drafting notes to assist in memory recall during our conversation.

The day of the interview came. The day of the interview dawned, and as the morning sun streamed through my windows, my heart oscillated between palpable nerves and bubbling excitement. Upon arrival, the interviewer, a distinguished-looking man named Dr. Ford, greeted me with a warm, reassuring smile, momentarily alleviating some of my anxiety.

As the questions began to flow, the initial knot in my stomach started to unravel. With each interview question, I reached for my crafted notes, responding with both confidence and an unexpected burst of creativity. With pride, I told them about my educational background, shared tales of my past experiences, and expressed my fervent passion for the pharmaceutical industry. My responses, woven with anecdotes from my past, underscored my adaptability and acute problem-solving skills.

After the preliminary questions, Dr. Ford, with an intrigued glint in his eyes, asked, "Ms. Wafula, can you share more about yourself? We're keen to understand the person behind this impressive resume."

With a deep breath, signifying my readiness, I replied. Instead of parroting a rehearsed, generic response, I opted to bear my soul. Delicately, I unearthed tales of my personal battles, especially the daunting shadow of amnesia that loomed large in my past. I emphasized the hurdles it imposed and how it deepened my appreciation for the fragile nature of memory and underscored the vital significance of pharmaceutical research.

The room was thick with emotion as they listened, their eyes shimmering with genuine empathy and interest. The resonance of my story was evident in their rapt attention. Taking this as encouragement, I treaded further into my past, elucidating the hurdles, the moments of triumph, and the profound personal evolution that had emerged from those trials.

When I finally finished, the room was heavy with silence. Then, a kind-hearted lady named Laura, her eyes now glistening with unshed tears, broke the stillness. "Thank you for baring your soul, Ms. Wafula," she said, her voice filled with admiration. "The challenges you've faced and surmounted require incredible resilience and courage. We have been on the lookout for an individual who possesses not only the requisite qualifications but also an indomitable spirit. Evidently, you embody both."

I could not believe what I was hearing. A flood of relief washed over me, making it feel like a weight had been lifted off my shoulders. Laura's voice filled the room with warmth as she continued, "Our company highly values diversity, and we genuinely believe that your unique background will offer a fresh perspective to our team."

At long last, I found interviewers who were not just impressed by my responses but were genuinely captivated by my unique perspective. It was evident that they were looking beyond my occasional memory lapses, recognizing instead the potential value I could bring to their esteemed organization.

As days turned into weeks, the anticipation built. Then, the call that marked a new chapter in my life finally arrived. Their words resonated with triumph, "We're offering you the job—a one-year contract position."

To say I was elated would be an understatement. It was the golden opportunity I had been waiting for, the perfect platform to showcase my skills and rekindle my passion for the industry. The ensuing wave of relief was overwhelming. The reality dawned that not only was I stepping back into employment, but I was also diving headfirst into an exciting, dynamic work environment. With renewed strength, I embarked on this fresh chapter of my career. I had the clarity that while memory might occasionally play its tricks, my determination and unwavering perseverance would stand steadfast. Life, with its countless challenges, often takes us by surprise. But it is our resilience, our ability to adapt, grow, and triumph, that truly charts our journey.

Embracing this spirit and the newfound opportunity, I plunged into my role with gusto. Determined to make a mark, I committed myself to proving that life's setbacks could not define my potential or eclipse my ambitions. As the days rolled on, I seamlessly blended into the hybrid work system, showcasing my prowess in remote team meetings and ingeniously collaborating with my colleagues.

The position was undeniably challenging. I was entrusted with the colossal task of setting up a Risk Management unit entirely from scratch. There was no manual or blueprint awaiting me; every step forward would require intuitive leaps. My past experiences told me that I had the skills and tenacity for such a task, so fueled by determination, I began. I delved deep into research, soaking up every bit of knowledge, and even reached out to industry gurus, hungry for their insights and guidance.

But the universe seemed intent on testing me even further. Beyond the difficult task of setting up the unit, there were associated projects demanding my attention. Working for a global conglomerate introduced the challenge of juggling time zones that spanned continents. Sunrises saw me already at my desk, and sunsets often bid me goodbye, marking long, grueling 12-hour days.

A pleasant surprise awaited me one morning, three months into my rigorous journey. With a twinkle of appreciation in his eyes, my manager relayed some heartwarming news. "Your dedication is evident in the work you've been delivering. The creativity and innovation you bring is truly commendable." This recognition, coming from a place of genuine appreciation, was the validation I needed. Every late night and early morning, every challenge I faced felt worth it. Emboldened by this vote of confidence, I faced challenges with renewed strength. I meticulously carved out objectives and weaved strategies to meet them. I built connections with industry experts and like-minded colleagues.

The months that followed were transformative. The Risk Management unit, once just a concept, began to manifest with clarity. I meticulously designed policies and procedures, ensuring a robust framework was in place to assess and shield the organization's assets from potential threats. The resounding success of the unit wasn't an accolade I could claim solely as my own, as it was proof of the tireless collaboration of every single team member.

Gratitude and accolades from senior management and peers alike became a familiar tune. With each pat on the back and word of appreciation, my chest swelled with pride, knowing the indelible mark I'd left on the organization. Our Risk Management unit wasn't just a cog in the machine - it had become a pivotal force, overseeing risk across all levels of the company's assets.

As the final pages of my contract began to turn, I found myself standing at life's crossroads before I lay a chance to cement a full-time position within the same firm that had seen me grow while other doors beckoned with opportunities in the vast realm of the biopharmaceutical industry. My heart was filled with gratitude for my time at the company, yet an irrepressible yearning existed to test new waters and set sail for uncharted territories.

The realm of biopharmaceuticals brimmed with an array of captivating roles and duties, each more alluring than the previous. However, amidst this sea of opportunities, it was the project management position at a particular company that truly captivated my attention. This enticing offer not only promised to carry forward my professional journey but also presented an opportunity to do different hats, acquire new knowledge, and flourish.

After nights of introspection, I chose to take the leap, signing on with the new company. I felt a whirlwind of emotions — excitement at the new adventure that awaited and a tinge of anxiety, leaving behind the familiarity I'd built at my previous job. But in my heart, I recognized this step as a launchpad to further personal and professional evolution.

From the moment I stepped into the buzzing atmosphere of the new office, a gut feeling assured me that I had made the right call. The aura of the workspace was vibrant and stimulating, but what truly struck a chord with me was the genuine warmth from every corner. These were not just colleagues — they felt like friends, mentors, allies. Above all, my manager shimmered like a guiding star amidst this constellation of supportive colleagues.

Her mentorship was invaluable. Drawing from her vast reservoir of knowledge, she introduced me to the nuanced world of project management, particularly its interplay with Risk Management. It was not just about the work; she invested time in understanding my aspirations and shaping my growth, both professionally and personally.

Each day spent learning from her, I experienced a revitalized motivation and self-assurance. The responsibilities assigned to me were not mere obligations anymore; they presented themselves as chances for growth and development. These tasks pushed me to enhance my problem-solving abilities, refine my communication techniques, and engage with a wide range of individuals in a meaningful way.

The work I was doing began to resonate deeply, reinforced by the affirmations from my manager and peers. My stride grew confident, and my projects expanded in scope and complexity. Every successful endeavor and every bit of positive feedback added fuel to my passion. Yet, lurking in the shadows was my struggle with amnesia, unpredictable and uncalled for. The demon that once held me captive had lost its sting. There were moments in the middle of a discussion when my thoughts would dissolve into nothingness.

I'd chuckle, saying, "Oops, my mind went blank again."

Instead of awkward silences or uncomfortable stares, my colleagues would smile understandingly, "It is okay. We all have those moments." Such affirmations dissolved any remnants of anxiety.

A dense fog of forgetfulness would roll in on certain days, making familiar tasks feel like insurmountable challenges. Yet, even on those days, a lifeline was always at hand. One such day, when a particular task's details eluded me, I reached out to Sarah. "Sarah, could you help me recall the details of this project?"

Always the epitome of patience, Sarah would sift through emails and notes, ensuring we pieced together the puzzle. Her support was a pillar of strength. Yet another peculiarity of my condition revealed itself – typos. It felt as if my fingers danced to their tune, sometimes out of rhythm with my thoughts. One day, I mentioned this to Linda, my manager, in a light-hearted moment. I remarked with a laugh, "Seems like my fingers are thinking a step ahead today, or maybe they're just on a different wavelength."

Linda's laughter echoed mine as she replied, "Oh, don't sweat it. We have all had those days. It is part of the charm!" Her jest and empathy transformed a potentially awkward moment into one of genuine bonds and friendship.

With time, I've come to realize that the support of my new work environment is not just limited to my colleagues. It extends to my supervisor, my manager, and even the company. They understand that conditions don't define a person or an employee. Instead, they see it as a unique aspect of diversity. It is truly reflective of the wonderful work culture we have built together. Over time, I have found strategies to cope with my memory lapses. From setting reminders on my phone to jotting down detailed notes, I've developed ways to offset the occasional slip-ups. Yet, I am reassured knowing that if I do forget, my colleagues are there as a safety net, gently reminding me of the things that momentarily eluded my grasp.

Through this journey of both self-discovery and self-acceptance, I've gathered profound insights. My amnesia, instead of being a restriction, has evolved into a catalyst for creativity. I now see unique solutions to problems, often identifying perspectives that might elude others. This fresh approach is valued by my colleagues, leading to new opportunities and collaborations. As a team, we tackle challenges and revel in our achievements, always aware that our strength is rooted in recognizing our differences and backing each other through all of life's hurdles.

Beyond the confines of the office, this newfound self-assurance has positively influenced my personal endeavors. Embracing fresh hobbies and interests, I'm no longer shackled by self-doubt or a fear of stumbling. My aspirations for financial stability, that sense of security that once seemed so elusive, are within reach. Thus, I was primed to continue my pursuit of turning these dreams into tangible reality.

However, life hurled an unexpected curveball my way. My medical hiatus meant a pause in my dreams. But now, it was time to press play. Determined, I walked into my bank, equipped with a proposal I believed would be my steppingstone to success. My plan was to transform my single-family home into a duplex, a project that would generate the additional income needed to expedite my goals. The initial bank I approached could not accommodate such projects. But rather than seeing this as a defeat, it made me more determined to seek an alternate route.

I delved into research with enthusiasm, gathering every piece of information I could find on financing options for real estate ventures. I spoke to experts in the field with keen interest, sought advice from experienced investors, and educated myself with dedication on the complexity of the real estate market. Armed with this newfound knowledge and a sense of hope, I began submitting numerous loan applications. However, each one was met with rejection due to the break in my career or lack of consistent income. I refused to let these rejections dampen my spirit. I persisted, believing that success was just around the corner.

Then, after what felt like an eternity of applications and tireless effort, I found a lender who saw the potential in my vision. They recognized my determination and the meticulous planning behind my project. With a sigh of relief, I secured the financing I needed to convert my home into a duplex.

As the renovation began, I was anxious. This was only the start of my journey toward financial stability. In the neighboring state, I've acquired property on a picturesque two-acre farm, which my family and I are passionately rehabbing into our dream home. Despite the exhausting work and seemingly endless days, each accomplishment pushes us closer to our dreams. I have also obtained three additional properties simultaneously, each brimming with aspirations of renovating and leasing them. The real estate industry, with its countless opportunities, has consistently fascinated me. I have voraciously absorbed all literature, publications, and workshops within reach, eager to expand my knowledge and achieve prosperity.

Naturally, there were occasions when uncertainty loomed, instances when time appeared to pass by swiftly. However, I remained determined not to allow valuable years to elude me, particularly after my medical hiatus. I drew inspiration from the metaphorical phrase "regain the years the locusts ate" from the Bible. It stirred emotions of renewal and recapturing lost time, and this notion became a guiding light in my personal voyage.

As the calendar eagerly flips to 2024, we are on track to complete the renovation of our cherished farmhouse and move in. The duplex renovation, imbued with anticipation, will be nearing its thrilling completion, and my vision to rent out the additional properties pulsates with promise.

I make a heartfelt promise to myself that this pursuit will not conclude here. I deeply understand that success isn't just a destination but a vibrant, ongoing journey. I take moments filled with gratitude to appreciate the milestones achieved, allowing myself a well-deserved, prideful pat on the back. Yet, with an invigorated spirit, I also gaze forward, setting my sights on new aspirations and vividly envisioning a horizon brimming with growth, prosperity, and enticing opportunities yet to unfurl.

On the family front, my eldest daughter, shining brightly at New York University, continues to excel. Driven by ambition, she remains focused on her goals as she earns recognition and secures scholarships. When presented with the opportunity to study abroad for a year, my heart was filled with mixed emotions. It dawned on me that she had never spread her wings away from the nest, and the overnight metamorphosis she'd have to undergo was both exhilarating and nerve-wracking.

Regrettably, circumstances constrained me from accompanying her during this monumental leap. With the weight of a fledgling career on my shoulders, adjusting to a new job consumed my focus. Our hearts ached from the distance, yet I saw a fierce determination in her. Carrying her bulky 100-pound suitcases and with her loyal cat, Leo, by her side, she courageously charted her path to London.

I experienced an overwhelming sense of joy during Thanksgiving and Christmas when I successfully obtained tickets for her, bringing her back to the loving embrace of our family. Although our reunion was brief, it filled my heart with happiness. For months, we had relied on phone calls and video chats to stay connected but seeing her in person was truly eye-opening. I was amazed by the remarkable personal growth she had undergone and how effortlessly she carried the weight of responsibility.

The moment I eventually set foot in London, witnessing her realm, emotions swirled. Observing her deftly navigate the city's maze and command her new life, pride welled within me. It was a defining moment, etching into my heart the undeniable fact that I had nurtured a fiercely independent and resilient gem.

On the other hand, my middle daughter, Elna, wrestled with the waves of change as she adjusted to college life. The heart-wrenching decision to switch colleges after merely one semester weighed on us. The battle to find her niche and balance academics with a quest for social belonging continued to challenge her spirit. But through every stumble and misstep, my unwavering support has been her anchor.

While Elna grappled with her journey, my younger two, Hadasha and Ethan, soared in their unique ways. Embracing their academic and extracurricular worlds with zeal, they've made strides both in studies and social circles. My heart swells with gratitude, and I find myself whispering thanks to the heavens for the richness of blessings and the robust support system encircling us.

The unwavering support from my partner has been a pillar of strength. His boundless creativity and poised knack for handling twists and turns have been our compass through the tumultuous seas of parenting. Hand in hand, we've fostered a nurturing haven where our children can spread their wings and chase their dreams.

Through the mosaic of challenges and victories, the unyielding constant has been the love and unshakable bond knitting our family. Embracing our roles as parents, we've imbibed that each child's odyssey is distinct, and occasionally, hurdles sculpt growth. Our steadfast presence, our cheers from the sidelines, and our rock-solid foundation empower them to rise.

I experience an overwhelming sense of pride deep within me when I reflect upon the unique qualities of my daughters and our cherished son. Their unwavering determination and commitment serve as a guiding light, inspiring a profound feeling of joy. They have a promising future ahead of them, and I eagerly await the unfolding of their extraordinary paths.

Thus, with a heart brimming with gratitude and a spirit infused with resolve, I've embarked on the next phase of my journey. Life has unveiled that it isn't solely about erecting structures or crafting processes, as mirrored in my project management role. It is a dance with challenges, a foray beyond familiar shores, and an undying thirst for excellence. The mountains that once towered over us have now transformed into steppingstones, guiding us towards personal growth and self-improvement.

Standing at the crossroads, I'm geared to confront the winds of tomorrow, fortified by lessons of yesteryears and an unflinching focus on my aspirations. Vision boards, for me, aren't mere collages; they're tangible dreams, beckoning reality. A conviction so profound I've sown its seeds in my daughters, urging them to sketch their visions and trust their heartbeats. These boards aren't just instruments; they're gateways to futures we passionately conjure.

With hope as my compass, I believe financial stability isn't a distant star; it is a milestone within my grasp. The same fervor, grit, and spirit that steered me thus far from my ambitions. The morrow beckons with mystery, and I'm eager for revelation. So, if ever doubt clouds your horizon or a giant stands defiant, recall my narrative. Harness your might, cherish every high and low, and honor the sanctity of your journey. For it is often in face-offs with titanic odds that we unearth buried might and unlock our boundless essence.

Chapter 14: Legacy

IN THE LIVELY STREETS OF AFRICA, surrounded by vibrant cultures and endless dreams, I once believed with all my heart that my legacy would be rooted in my homeland. Little did I know, to my surprise, that my path would take me across oceans and continents, shaping who I am and redefining my life's purpose.

Over a decade ago, with a deep breath and hope in my eyes, I took a leap of faith and left my secure corporate job in Africa behind. With only a few dollars in my pocket and no clear direction in mind, I embarked on a challenging journey toward the shores of the United States. The whispers of opportunity, a better life, and the promise of untold stories lured me into the unknown.

Those initial days, heavy with nostalgia, were filled with uncertainty and vulnerability. Is this the right choice? Can I make it here? I found solace in the confines of a modest hotel room, where the flickering neon lights outside mirrored the flickering thoughts within my mind. As I stood at the crossroads of my past and future, the African diaspora community shared with me their valuable advice, although some misguided me, much to my disappointment.

Moved by a longing for connection and a hint of loneliness, I decided to leave behind the solitude of the hotel and took refuge in the warm embrace of a host family. They graciously opened their doors and hearts to me, teaching me the strength of shared humanity. This feels like home.

With their support and words of encouragement, I found the courage to face the adversities that lay ahead. Through perseverance and an unyielding determination, with sweat on my brow and hope in my stride, I began to carve my path in this foreign land. From working minimum-wage jobs to learning the dynamics of corporate America, I embraced every opportunity that presented itself, often with a mixture of trepidation and excitement.

The learning curves were steep, and failures, like bitter pills, were plentiful, but I refused to let them define me. Instead, they became steppingstones, pushing me toward a future veiled in success. However, with its unpredictable turns, life presented me with unforeseen challenges. In the midst of my pursuit of the American dream, I was dealt a devastating blow, like a sharp intake of breath – a diagnosis of cancer. Why now? Why me? The tendrils of fear wrapped tightly around my heart, threatening to choke every ounce of hope from my being. The battle against cancer was difficult, filled with countless treatments and their brutal side effects. One of the cruelest consequences of my fight was the onset of amnesia, a thief who silently and cruelly stole fragments of my past, my memories, and my identity.

Like an artist starting with a blank canvas, I had to relearn my own story and build a fresh foundation. A newfound clarity emerged as I painstakingly pieced together the remnants of my forgotten past. It made me realize that my legacy would not be bound by the familiar lands I once called home. I do hope that my legacy one day will transcend borders, touch lives, and ignite a flame of inspiration in others through resilience and determination.

So, dear reader, as I pen down these words with a heavy heart and earnest hope, my reason for leaving a legacy became clear.

It was not merely about the corporate successes or the grueling battles against cancer but the undeniable fact that I stood tall against the tide, defied the odds and refused to let circumstances define or diminish me.

I yearned to be remembered for plunging headfirst into the unknown, for crossing vast oceans and continents with a heart full of dreams, and for rising, Phoenix-like, from the ashes of adversity, time and time again. My purpose? My legacy would scream the message that irrespective of our roots or the daunting mountains we face. We harness an innate power for greatness. At the twilight of my journey, this legacy would stand as a shining witness to the power of unyielding hope and the indomitable spirit of the human soul.

What is a story without its most profound characters? My legacy would have no narrative without the resounding laughter and enduring tears of my children interwoven into its chapters. In this land overflowing with aspirations and limitless possibilities, just like any unfolding tale, survival became our shared anthem. Side by side, my children and I confronted the storm, bearing witness to the raw realities of life, where we experienced the bitter-sweet essence of its shadows and radiance.

Our lives operated like a finely tuned clock, centered around a precise routine, where my children took on responsibilities that exceeded their young age. When the school bell chimed, marking the conclusion of yet another day, my children would hasten back home, fully aware of the need to care for their younger sibling, while I hurriedly headed off to work.

Each missed shift meant sacrificing a part of our meager income, leaving us struggling to make ends meet. There were days when I failed to clock in on time and was sent home without pay, bearing a heavy heart burdened by financial strain. Though circumstances weighed us down, my children displayed a resilience that belied their age. They matured overnight, carrying burdens far beyond what children should bear. But amid the chaos and hardships, I was determined to give them hope and purpose.

I sought refuge in a small church, where I poured my heart out in songs filled with dreams and aspirations. Within the walls of that humble sanctuary, I discovered a fellowship, unlike anything I had experienced before. Fellow immigrants who understood the struggles and challenges of being in a foreign land embraced us with open arms. Together, we formed a tight-knit community, bound together by perseverance and an unwavering determination to never give up.

Despite the lack of material possessions, I held onto my dreams fiercely. My vision board, adorned with pictures depicting endless possibilities and uncharted journeys, encapsulated my boundless imagination. It served as a wellspring of motivation, constantly reminding me that life held more than just our present hardships. Even during moments when the world appeared unyielding, my dreams softly murmured assurances of a radiant tomorrow.

Slowly but surely, I began to plant the seeds of change in the hearts and minds of my children. As we gathered around our small dinner table each night, I shared tales of courage, resilience, and ambition. I painted vivid pictures of what life could be like if we held onto our dreams and nurtured them with unwavering determination. Day by day, my children's young hearts soaked up these tales, and the seeds of ambition began to grow within their souls. They started to have faith in their ability to conquer any challenge that life presented to them.

As I pen this, I am amazed by the incredible achievements of my children, who have surpassed all my expectations with their hard work, dedication, and fearless determination. Each of them is blazing their own trail, driven by their individual talents and passions.

As I look into their eyes, I see a spark of hope and a belief in a brighter tomorrow that inspires me. Watching them grow and thrive over the years, excelling in their studies and pursuing their dreams, fills me with immense pride and happiness. I cannot wait to see what the future holds for them as they continue to weave their unique stories into the fabric of our family's legacy.

One stands on the cusp of medicine, poised to heal and transform lives. Another is into technology, intent on leaving an indelible mark on our digital interactions. Yet the other dives into the depths of the arts, crafting beauty destined to resonate with countless souls.

Hand in hand, we've shattered expectations and toppled the barriers that dared to hinder us. People often express awe at the monumental growth of my family, once intimately acquainted with strife. I have hopes that our narrative might serve as a guide for others, motivating them to chase their dreams regardless of daunting odds.

Reflecting upon our shared odyssey, it is evident to me that the legacy I yearn to bestow isn't anchored in tangible riches or acquisitions and material possessions. It is a legacy of strength and unwavering determination in the face of adversity. It is built on aspirations and fueled by creative passion—a firm belief that with enough determination, even the most daunting obstacles can be overcome.

I yearn for remembrance as a mother who planted the seeds of dreams in her children, who bolstered their spirits during difficult moments, reminding them of their inner fortitude. May our shared journey stand as an enduring reminder of human resilience, emphasizing that no challenge is too towering if one dares to dream and labor relentlessly toward it.

My children, who once shouldered hefty responsibilities, now shine as pillars of hope. I wish for them to pass on the essence of our legacy to the forthcoming generations, ensuring our narrative remains timeless.

The legacy I seek to leave is one that celebrates tenacity, determination, and an unwavering belief in dreams. It is a message that knows no borders, resonating with the tireless spirit in each of us.

"What legacy would I leave behind?" I wondered again. Then, it dawned on me: No topic is off-limits. Let's talk about mental health. In a world where silence hangs like a dense fog, where invisible chains of societal judgment hold us back, it is important to remember that sharing our struggles, especially the ones we face within our own minds, should never be a cause for shame. I strive to be a guiding light for mental health, shedding light on the once taboo and misunderstood, offering a glimmer of hope for those who feel trapped in their silent pain.

The burden of judgment was a familiar restraint that I carried, paralyzed by the overwhelming fear of being seen as a failure or weak. The barriers surrounding me appeared impenetrable, trapping me within their confines. However, little did I know that my passage through the labyrinth of the psychiatric ward would signify the commencement of a courageous and determined legacy.

As I hesitantly stepped into that unit not so long ago, I felt a deluge of shame engulf me. Stripped of my personal freedoms, every movement was monitored. Even the most harmless items, like shoelaces, were viewed with suspicion and swiftly removed. *Did they really think I'd create an escape using just a string?* The sheer absurdity of the notion stung. Could they not see I was there seeking help, not an escape route?

We lined up, mouths open, as we swallowed our daily doses of pills. Obediently, we allowed staff to inspect our mouths to prove that meds were swallowed. *Is this what it had come to?* However, in the depths of that darkness, I found solace. Surrounded by those who shared my battle, I realized the shame I had carried was not mine to bear alone. I left that place forever changed, armed with a resolve to challenge society's perception of mental health.

My legacy, I vowed, would be one of unwavering honesty and compassion. No longer would I hide in the shadows, silenced by shame. *"I have to speak out."* For myself. For others. I would use the power of my voice to demolish the walls that confined us. Surrounded by a community of survivors and warriors who emerged from the darkness, I found solace in our shared battle scars. Through our social media group, we share art, music, and words of encouragement. We have crafted hope and resilience, vulnerably sharing our stories.

The legacy I aspire to leave is not merely a story of triumph over mental illness, for the battles continue within. It is a legacy of unity, echoing the fact that seeking help is courageous. It reminds everyone that our stories, raw and sometimes jarring, hold the power to inspire healing.

So, let's discuss legacy, with no subject off limits because in the darkest moments, when one might feel alone, there's an inherent power within us all to rise, advocate, and craft a world more receptive to mental health.

Speaking of health, I will bear my truth. Following the various chemical treatments, I noticed a significant increase in my weight. I was constantly battling to shed those extra pounds, but it seemed like an impossible task. Each visit to the doctor filled me with fear and frustration. With every pound added, I received a rebuke from the doctor – "Ms. Wafula, you need to lose more weight. Your blood pressure is edging up!"

The cycle of despair never ended, and I grew averse to doctor visits. The constant reminders of my weight struggles made me feel like a failure. I longed for someone who would understand my pain and offer a solution rather than dictating my life and making me feel even worse about myself. *Is it too much to ask for some empathy?*

My personal doctor reappeared on the scene after a three-year hiatus. She looked at me with compassion and studied the long list of medications on my chart. With determination in her eyes, she said, "Ms. Wafula, we are going to fix this together. I want you back to your old self."

I could not believe what I was hearing. Is this the turning point I've been waiting for? Tears of gratitude welled up in my eyes as I realized someone finally understood the depths of my struggle. I had grown tired of people telling me what to do and how heavy I had become. Enough is enough. It is time to take my health into my own hands.

I decided to embark on a new journey. Once I secured a job, I dedicated my spare time to researching a unique option - medical tourism. I discovered that many Americans were traveling abroad for their medical needs, including weight-loss surgeries. I became particularly intrigued by bariatric surgery, seeing it as a potential game-changer in my life.

With an open mind and a renewed sense of hope, I packed my bags and headed to Mexico. There, I met a friendly and knowledgeable medical professional, Emily, and her sister, Sarah, who worked as a nurse. Coincidentally, they were also in Mexico for the same reason - to undergo bariatric surgery. Maybe this journey isn't so lonely after all.

I knew I was taking control of my life, doing what made me happy, and striving for a healthier future. Months passed, and the transformation within me has been incredible. I have lost a significant amount of weight and regained my confidence, and my high blood pressure is now a thing of the past. More importantly, I had discovered my legacy - to take control of my life and do what makes me truly happy, embracing self-love and the pursuit of well-being.

I am an advocate for self-empowerment and prioritizing personal well-being. I share my story with friends, family, and even strangers, encouraging them to explore options beyond their comfort zones. I have realized that taking control of our health sometimes means stepping outside the boundaries and norms imposed by others.

It means having the courage to make unconventional choices and find happiness in our own unique ways. I hope to inspire others to break free from societal expectations and take charge of their destinies. I lost weight, yes, but more importantly, I found myself again, reclaiming my health and rewriting my own story.

As my life's chapter continues to unfold, I'm determined to ink each page with dedication and love. Every day shapes my legacy, not by the setbacks I face but by the spirit I show confronting them. When my time on this earth concludes, I hope my story touches those close to me and those brave enough to chase their dreams, no matter the obstacles.

Adversity has never fazed me. I've stared down death more times than I can count. As a teenager, a motor accident left me with a compression fracture. The prognosis was grim, but I rose up. Even with lost memories, I rallied, reclaiming what was mine, and even aced my college exams. Every challenge is just another story of triumph waiting to be written.

They say lightning doesn't strike twice in the same spot, but fate had something else in store for me. Years later, I lost my memory again, this time due to ECT treatment for depression. It was a painful journey, but I did not let it break me. I rose stronger, always pushing forward, determined to overcome every obstacle that crossed my path.

Fast forward to the day when I had landed my dream corporate America job. I was so diligent and dedicated that not even a snowstorm could keep me away from work. Despite the treacherous roads and slow progress, I decided to drive. My GPS kept rerouting me, searching for the "best route" amidst the chaos.

Lost on an unfamiliar road, I felt panic rising within me. Suddenly, my vehicle started skidding downhill, helpless against the slippery snow. It was as if time had slowed down, and I knew the inevitable was about to happen. As the distance passed between my car and this massive tree, I closed my eyes and said my last prayers.

When I opened my eyes, the scene before me was surreal. The front of my SUV was barely inches away from an imposing tree. Miraculously, nothing was broken, and I was entirely unscathed. Breathing heavily, I fumbled for my phone, dialing my boss. "You would not believe what just happened. My car... it is right in front of a tree. But I'm okay!"

As my heart raced, I dialed my ex-husband. "I had an accident. Can you come? I think I'm fine, but I could use some help."

Before long, a good Samaritan stopped by, anchoring a rope to my SUV, attempting to pull it away from its position. "It is not moving!" He called out, with frustration in his voice.

My ex-husband pulled up, concern in his eyes. "Are you okay?" he asked, surveying the scene. We tried to maneuver the car, but our efforts were in vain.

Feeling a mix of despair and hope, I called my partner. "My SUV is literally nosing a tree. I don't know what to do!"

A few tense minutes later, a police vehicle pulled up at the scene. An officer stepped out, casting a professional gaze over the situation. He walked around the tree, taking in every detail. After a moment, he approached me, pointing to the ground. "You see these rocks?" He pointed at two large stones nestled in the snow on either side of the tree. "I believe they stopped your car's tires from hitting the tree. You're very lucky."

Chills ran down my spine as the realization hit. Those random rocks might have just saved my life for whatever reason they were there. Funny enough, the officer himself had been a geography major. It was his keen eye that had recognized these rocks as something more than they seemed. He called them "Canadian life rocks" or something like that, explaining that they had been transplanted from elsewhere.

I was completely stunned - the odds of such a perfect alignment of circumstances seemed too unlikely. How could these stones be there in that exact spot, precisely when I needed them the most? It felt like a divine intervention. I could have easily met my end that day, but fate had a different plan for me.

I imagined the course of my car, moving toward the massive tree that now stood untouched. Had it not been for those rocks, I would have collided with the tree, ending in a devastating crash. It was a chilling thought. Fate had intervened, sparing me from a tragic end. But why? What was the purpose behind this extraordinary coincidence?

Deep down, I knew life was full of mysteries beyond our comprehension. Perhaps this incident was a gentle reminder that there were forces at work, forces we could not fully understand or control. It was a humbling experience, reminding me of the fragility and preciousness of life.

Since that incident, I have come to realize that we all have a purpose in life. I keep the police report from that fateful day as a reminder of the fragility of life and the power of resilience. Every time I look at it, I'm reminded of the greater forces at play, a reminder of the infinite possibilities hidden beneath our existence.

Life may throw adversities our way, but it is up to us to stand tall, face them head-on, and emerge victorious. I carry this lesson with me, forever grateful for the second chances I have been granted. We must be ready to embrace the everyday miracles that come our way, even if they arrive in the form of seemingly mundane Canadian life rock.

As a person, I have my non-negotiable beliefs carved deep into my soul. I have long learned that we are all unique beings, each with a different purpose in life. These are the guiding principles that have shaped my journey and continue to inspire me to live life on my own terms.

"Live your life for your own," I remind myself every morning as I embrace the new day. Our existence is a precious gift, and it is our responsibility to find our true selves and follow our passion. It is living authentically, honoring our desires, and embracing the freedom to be who we truly are.

"Live for today. Tomorrow is not given" is a constant mantra that resonates in every heartbeat. Life is fleeting and unpredictable. We must cherish each present moment, squeezing out every drop of joy, love, and fulfillment before the day slips away. It is a reminder to enjoy the beauty of life and leave no room for regrets.

"If you get no for an answer, learn why it is a no" is a seed of curiosity firmly planted in my mind. Rejection is not the end but rather an opportunity for introspection. I use the opportunity to delve deeper into the reasons behind each refusal, gaining valuable insights to improve and make a stronger case or comeback. With resilience and determination, I knock on the doors of opportunity, confident that one will surely open.

"Live your dreams, even if it means faking it until it happens," I whisper as I channel my inner courage. You see, dreams are the fuel that propels us forward, even in the face of uncertainty. Sometimes, the path to our dreams may require stepping outside our comfort zone and pretending until we make it a reality. In doing so, we infuse our dreams with unwavering dedication.

"Have a purpose, even if you don't have a dollar for it" is a reminder that true fulfillment lies not in wealth but in meaning. Money may come and go, but the purpose remains everlasting. I embrace the power of passion and determination, understanding that purpose is not limited by financial resources. With unwavering clarity, I create a vision board, outlining my aspirations and infusing each goal with intention.

"Gratitude" is my daily companion, a source of solace and strength. It anchors me during life's turbulent times, serving as a constant reminder that nothing is taken personally. While our situations may put us to the test, we can alter our outlook by nurturing gratitude and uncovering beauty even within the difficulties. It serves as a perpetual prompt to value the intricacies of each moment, regardless of their simplicity or profundity.

Finally, "Be a positive contribution to a place, a person, or a thing." By radiating positivity, kindness, and love, we become catalysts for change, touching lives and making the world brighter. It is in this selfless contribution that we find purpose beyond ourselves. The non-negotiable beliefs I cherish serve as the compass for my life's journey. They fuel my spirit, reminding me that I hold the pen that writes my destiny with every breath. I harness the power of creativity, crafting my life's narrative with every heartbeat of passion and an undying commitment to leave a meaningful imprint.

Life's journey isn't always straight. It is similar to a winding river with its unexpected bends and turns, sometimes leading to uncharted waters. Through time, I've understood that boundaries like age, location, and time are merely illusions. Every individual holds the power to pivot, to redirect their life's path, whenever and wherever they feel the pull.

The key lies in embracing change, channeling resilience, and harnessing determination. It is important to face the challenges life presents, derive strength from shared experiences, and uplift others by bearing witness to your own story.

With each day, my heart swells with love, my career path shines brighter, and my entrepreneurial spirit in the realm of real estate finds new vigor.

I know what it is like to be a single mother, but I also know what it is like to find love again! Through it all, I remain grateful for the extraordinary life I have lived - a testament to three things: The power of love (even when it doesn't work out), determination (even when it seems futile), and self-belief (even when others doubt).

In the end, it is not the destination that matters most but the journey we undertake and the profound impact we have on the lives we touch. This is the legacy I strive to leave behind, a legacy that reminds the world that anything is possible if we believe in ourselves and dare to create our own destinies.

Chapter 15: Today and Tomorrow

AS I REFLECT ON THE winding journey of my life, captured in the pages of this memoir, a mix of emotions flood through me. Each chapter captures key moments and deep memories, immortalizing my odyssey of love, loss, adversity, and triumph.

In reliving these vivid scenes from my past, I am reminded of the absolute resilience of the human spirit. My story bears witness to the incredible inner strength that lies resting until called upon in our darkest hours. I have navigated treacherous storms, from wrestling with illness and memory loss to overcoming relationship turmoil and financial instability. Yet with every storm surge that threatened to capsize me, I discovered untapped wells of grit and determination, rising up stronger than before.

While my battles may have been unique, I know in my heart that we all face our own personal challenges. Some conflicts rage loudly like thunder; others are silent like a gathering storm. But we are bound by the currents of humanity that connect us. My wish is that within these pages, you find your struggles, your own courage, and glimmers of the undying hope we each carry. In between the twists and turns, there were breaks of profound joy and blessings that made the journey worthwhile. These short-lived yet magical moments are engraved in my spirit, reminding me to embrace life's ups and downs. So it is, with life, darkness, and light coexisting.

My mission in crafting this memoir came from a longing to share my truth, to lay bare my vulnerabilities, my scars, my dreams, and my essence. In these pages, you witnessed me struggling with myself and the world around me. You glimpsed into my lowest valleys and highest peaks. You bore witness as I peeled away the layers and found my voice.

I sought to honor the courage of human experience to emphasize that we need not travel this winding road alone. In sharing my unfiltered narrative, without pretenses, I hoped to spark self-reflection, reassurance, and the realization that, irrespective of our diverse backgrounds, we are united in our humanity.

There were moments when I hesitated, wondering if my story deserved to be told. Did my experiences offer any value to human narratives that echo across continents? Could my voice make an impact amidst the maelstrom of a million others?

Ultimately, I came to terms with the idea that significance lies not in fame or glory but in meaning, purpose, and sharing our true selves. So, with faith, I embraced the power of storytelling, understanding that changing even one life has a profound impact. I found my reason in inspiring others who feel silenced or cast aside, reminding them that their voices deserve to be heard, their dreams matter, and their existence is meaningful.

If these chapters resonated in your spirit, awakened your empathy, or provided you comfort in knowing you are not alone, then every word was worth it. If my peaks and valleys mirrored yours, validating your challenges, then this memoir served its purpose.

Your connection was the force that fueled my perseverance. So, as I guide this book toward its concluding pages, I wish to focus on the present that anchors me and the horizons that await. For woven into our pasts are important lessons that transform our today and empower our tomorrow.

As I take a pause from the rigors of narrating my memoir, life's vibrant hues seem even more pronounced before my eyes. Simplicity resonates—the charm of bare feet nestled in soft grass, the lyrical trill of birdsong, and the soothing fragrance of earth after rain. A renewed cognizance of life's fragile beauty resonates within me.

My children's laughter, once silenced by hardship, now echoes freely, filling our home with joyful music. Their dreams, unburdened by limitations, grow richer with the passage of time. In their eyes, I see reflections of my youthful innocence from a lifetime ago in Africa's sun-drenched savannah. Back then, my heart brimmed with starry-eyed plans, never once imagining how life's tides would sweep me far beyond home's horizon.

Standing here decades later, an ocean away from my birthplace, I am reminded that destiny blazes its trail. The seeds of hope planted long ago have blossomed into realities my younger self could only fantasize about. Hardships were transformed into footings of strength. Today, I am blessed to witness my children unfurl their wings and chase their visions of grandeur.

As I pen these words, I do so while enveloped in the warmth of true love, a peace I never imagined finding after life's storms. Yet fate deems it fit to gift us with small miracles when we least expect them. They remind us to embrace joy when it crosses our paths. After my tempestuous relationship experiences, I resolved that my heart would lay fallow, focusing solely on nurturing my family and realizing my ambitions.

Yet, an enigmatic gentleman walked into my life just as I was exiting an abusive relationship. Our first encounter had a hint of subtle friction, for his self-assurance rattled my wounds. Little did I know this unintended meeting would blossom into an extraordinary romance, teaching me that love inhabits endless embodiments.

It was not the fairy tale sort that fueled naïve fantasies. Instead, it was one steeped in understanding, acceptance, and allowing our scars to speak. He became my hand to hold when memories faded, my voice of reason amidst the chaos, my compass when the road ahead seemed unclear. Our affection flourished in the most unlikely conditions. During chemotherapy, his unwavering support became my lifeline, reminding me that I was never alone.

Our synergy worked its magic, forging an unbreakable bond, whether cradling me post-surgery or patiently decoding my misspoken words. Through his nurturing devotion and my commitment to unconditional love, our fractured pieces molded flawlessly together, crafting a mosaic of resilience. One by one, the closed doors of my heart creaked open, allowing light to alight once more.

Our affection embodies the remarkable capacity of love to renew itself, a celestial blaze that dances with renewed brightness and valor. Hand in hand, with synced heartbeats, we model for our children that love is not finite. Its magic endures beyond grief and disappointment. When nurtured honestly, love entwines souls in profound ways, lending strength for the journey ahead.

Beyond the gift of true love, I have been blessed on my quest with friendships that blossomed like wildflowers amidst storms. Their compassion saw me through tempestuous times when my inner light had dimmed. The bonds we share transcend the realms of age, culture, or status. Our hearts' truths speak a universal language that requires no translation.

Whether rejoicing in my triumphs or nursing me through chemotherapy's tolls, my community of kindred spirits lifted me higher. During my incarceration in psychiatric wards, their loyalty never faltered. They became my tethers to sanity and living reminders that I was never alone, even in my darkest moments of disconnect.

My dearest confidants were angels in disguise, arriving in my most desperate hours of need. Some offered shelter from homelessness; others shared wise counsel that has shaped my trajectory. The unwavering support of those I hold dear has been the nurturing balm that healed my spirit and reignited my aspirations. Their imprint on my existence remains indelible.

Professionally, I stand poised to unfurl my wings and renew my flight after having withdrawn into my cocoon. During my hiatus from corporate life, I realized that my passions stretch beyond the confines of one industry. I discerned that the diversity of my interests need not be constrained to just a single career vessel.

Like tributaries flowing into a great river, I understood that progress often involves exploring varied terrains before arriving at the sea of one's calling. This realization has been liberating, freeing me from the shackles of convention. I am determined to craft an unconventional career—more of a calling—that quenches my thirst for innovation.

Already, I have taken bold steps, venturing into the domain of entrepreneurship. Driven by my appetite for challenge and a vision to mold my destiny, I delved into real estate. Despite initial setbacks, I persevered, educating myself extensively and networking with experts. At long last, the seeds of my efforts have begun to bear fruit. I now stand proud as an investor, overseeing a growing portfolio of properties. This lays the foundation, providing financial security and flexibility to immerse myself in other dynamic projects.

As I reflect on my entrepreneurial journey thus far, I am reminded of the burdens borne by visionaries and innovators. Our dreams are often born as fragile ideas, requiring nurturing support and unwavering courage to manifest. My mission moving forward is to uplift other audacious minds, providing mentorship and opportunities to accelerate their growth.

I wish to assemble a collaboration of dynamic innovators, preferably people of the diaspora, with whom I can brainstorm and partner to birth inventive solutions worldwide. Be it addressing healthcare inequality, bridging the education gap, or developing sustainable technologies, I aim to be a conduit for change. Mine is a restless spirit devoted to harnessing creativity's power to inspire progress and impact on an international scale.

I hope to immerse myself in forwarding social change while leveraging my business acumen to amplify access and resources.

My own disjointed career trajectory has ignited a passion for empowering non-traditional talent and reassuring them that their unconventional paths matter. Having once felt sidelined myself, I am devoted to illuminating the limitless potential that lies beyond cultural and systemic labels. If I can plant seeds of hope in even one fellow changemaker, then I have succeeded in leaving an enduring legacy.

So, my voyage continues, navigating new tides but with a familiar rhythm. The seasons have changed, yet my dreams persist unabated. The world is rife with suffering and inequality, but my spirit remains unbroken. With the credibility afforded by my struggles, I am compelled to give back and pay my blessings forward.

Mine are dreams birthed from hope, carved from vision, and brought to life through tenacity. These aspirations course through my veins, yearning for purpose. Though my ambitions may seem lofty in their scope, I ground them in Mahatma Gandhi's wisdom, which reminds me, "Be the change you wish to see in the world."

On the horizon, I envision a future where innovators flourish unhindered, shaping society for the betterment of all. I see an era where inclusive policies tear down the walls that divide talent. Education transcends privilege, enriching communities that have only known scarcity. As I peer at the landscape ahead, I see people of all origins standing shoulder to shoulder, empowered to manifest their highest selves. This is the reality I endeavor to help create in ways big and small. By adding my voice to the collective song of change, I hope to inspire others to do the same. The world ahead remains unwritten, awaiting our hands to craft its narrative. So, with purpose as my compass, I embrace the present and welcome the future. I conclude this memoir with immense gratitude etched in my spirit. To everyone who accompanied me along the way through kind words, compassionate actions, or silent prayers, I thank you. You helped transform my breakdowns into breakthroughs. This book emerged from the faith you ignited in me, substantiating that each voice rings with purpose.

To you, dear reader, I am indebted for taking this reflective expedition by my side. By investing your time to peer into the landscapes of my life, you became part of my journey. It is my hope that you find reassurance and comfort in a story that echoes the universality of our shared human experiences. May we all seek opportunities to uplift one another, to speak our truth, and to leave this world a little brighter.

The final word I wish to impart is that life, for all its uncertainties, is profoundly beautiful. It is not defined merely by fleeting moments of joy or sadness but by our collective courage to face storms and yet never submit. Within us all lies the untapped potential for resilience and excellence. Let us have faith to explore the unknown, boldness to proclaim our truths, and wisdom to find fulfillment in our authentic journeys.

My life shall mirror these convictions until my sunset arrives. When that day comes, I hope I can rest easy, knowing that I left my mark by daring greatly, loving unconditionally, and inspiring change. For now, I embrace the gift that is today, bask in the community I am blessed with, and prepare for the opportunities that tomorrow shall bring. Onward and upward, always! This is my story.

www.ingramcontent.com/pod-product-compliance
Lightning Source LLC
Chambersburg PA
CBHW070755160726
48004CB00001B/195